Apache Maven Cookbook

Over 90 hands-on recipes to successfully build and
automate development life cycle tasks following Maven
conventions and best practices

Raghuram Bharathan

BIRMINGHAM - MUMBAI

Apache Maven Cookbook

First published: April 2015

Production reference: 1240415

Published by Packt Publishing Ltd.
Livery Place
35 Livery Street
Birmingham B3 2PB, UK.

ISBN 978-1-78528-612-4

www.packtpub.com

Credits

Author

Raghuram Bharathan

Reviewers

Gurkan Erdogdu

Jérôme Leleu

Peter Major

Phani Krishna Pemmaraju

Commissioning Editor

Ashwin Nair

Acquisition Editor

Vinay Argekar

Content Development Editor

Vaibhav Pawar

Technical Editors

Mrunal M. Chavan

Rahul C. Shah

Copy Editors

Sonia Michelle Cheema

Shambhavi Pai

Stuti Srivastava

Laxmi Subramanian

Project Coordinator

Kranti Berde

Proofreaders

Stephen Copestake

Safis Editing

Paul Hindle

Indexer

Tejal Soni

Production Coordinator

Alwin Roy

Cover Work

Alwin Roy

About the Author

Raghuram Bharathan is a postgraduate in computer applications from the National Institute of Technology, Trichy. In his career in the software industry, he has worked with Hewlett-Packard, Cisco, and ThoughtWorks, among others. He is the cofounder of Innoventes Technologies, a tech company involved in product engineering and providing services in mobile and web applications.

He is experienced in enterprise web and mobile technologies and is well-versed in the setting up, maintenance, and usage of various build automation tools, such as ANT, Apache Maven, Gradle, and Buildr.

He has been using Apache Maven for more than 7 years in his projects and is one of the top providers of answers for Maven in Stack Overflow.

About the Reviewers

Gurkan Erdogdu is the CTO and cofounder of MechSoft Software Solutions, based in Turkey. He has been working with Java™ and Java™ EE technologies since 1999. He is a member of several open source foundations, including Apache Software Foundation and OW2 Consortium. He is founder of the Apache OpenWebBeans and OW2 Siwpas open source projects. He holds a bachelor's degree in computer engineering from Middle East Technical University (METU). He lives in Istanbul with his wife and little daughter and can be reached at gurkanerdogdu@yahoo.com.

> I am thankful to my family, who have provided me with encouragement, friendship, wisdom, and patience throughout my life. Without them, it would not have been possible for me to become the person I am now.

Jérôme Leleu is a software architect living in Paris, France.

A consultant for 7 years, he has worked for many different companies in different fields and with a variety of people. He has participated in many IT projects as a developer, technical lead, or projects manager, though mostly in the J2EE technology.

Currently working in a French telecom company, he is the software architect of a WebSSO, which supports very high traffic: millions of authentications from millions of users everyday.

He is involved in open source development as a CAS (WebSSO) chairman. He's interested in security/protocol issues, and has developed several libraries (refer to http://www.pac4j.org) to implement client support for protocols such as CAS, OAuth, and OpenID.

He is the founder of an SSO Cloud provider, which is based on CAS (refer to https://www.casinthecloud.com).

Peter Major is a software developer at ForgeRock, where he has mainly been working on OpenAM, an enterprise scale single sign-on solution. In the past 5 years, he has worked on various Maven projects of divergent sizes and has been through the different stages of software development, testing, and release.

Phani Krishna Pemmaraju has more than 10 years of IT experience with expertise in SOA, ESB, J2EE/Spring technologies, mobile computing, and Oracle Fusion Middleware products. He completed his master's degree in computer applications as a topper from Osmania University, India. He has rich implementation expertise in EAI/SOA integrations and has worked on some challenging projects across different verticals.

He has extensive experience in architecting, designing, developing, and testing solutions using various SOA technology (SCA/JBI) products, such as Oracle Fusion, Java CAPS, and Glassfish ESB. He has worked for highly reputed IT consulting companies and various prestigious clients and played a key role in architecting and designing solutions. He has a penchant for learning new technologies and their implementation methodologies.

Thanks to Packt Publishing for giving me the opportunity to review this book and share my experiences and knowledge of Maven.

www.PacktPub.com

Support files, eBooks, discount offers, and more

For support files and downloads related to your book, please visit www.PacktPub.com.

Did you know that Packt offers eBook versions of every book published, with PDF and ePub files available? You can upgrade to the eBook version at www.PacktPub.com and as a print book customer, you are entitled to a discount on the eBook copy. Get in touch with us at service@packtpub.com for more details.

At www.PacktPub.com, you can also read a collection of free technical articles, sign up for a range of free newsletters and receive exclusive discounts and offers on Packt books and eBooks.

https://www2.packtpub.com/books/subscription/packtlib

Do you need instant solutions to your IT questions? PacktLib is Packt's online digital book library. Here, you can search, access, and read Packt's entire library of books.

Why Subscribe?

- ▶ Fully searchable across every book published by Packt
- ▶ Copy and paste, print, and bookmark content
- ▶ On demand and accessible via a web browser

Free Access for Packt account holders

If you have an account with Packt at www.PacktPub.com, you can use this to access PacktLib today and view 9 entirely free books. Simply use your login credentials for immediate access.

Table of Contents

Preface

Apache Maven Cookbook describes the features of Apache Maven through a series of recipes. This book will help you understand what Apache Maven is and allow you to use its features with the help of complete and working examples.

What this book covers

Chapter 1, Getting Started, covers the installation of Apache Maven on Microsoft Windows, Mac OS X, or Linux, as well as creating and building your first project with it. The chapter also details the steps to install prerequisite software required for Maven.

Chapter 2, IDE Integration with Maven, focuses on configuring popular IDEs with the help of Maven and running Maven projects in them. Eclipse, NetBeans, and IntelliJ IDEA are the three IDEs covered in this chapter.

Chapter 3, Maven Lifecycle, covers the life cycle of Apache Maven and explores the concept of phases and goals. It also describes how a user can use profiles to customize builds.

Chapter 4, Essential Maven Plugins, describes the Maven plugins, which are essential to build a project. For each plugin, the various configuration options are also explored.

Chapter 5, Dependency Management, explores the various types of Maven dependencies, and delves into downloading and getting reports on them. It also talks about how to handle network issues during a dependency download.

Chapter 6, Code Quality Plugins, covers the support provided for various code quality tools, such as Checkstyle, PMD, FindBugs, and Sonar. The configuration options for each plugin as well as generating reports are also explored.

Chapter 7, Reporting and Documentation, covers the reporting features of Maven. The site plugins and the various reports supported by it are described in detail.

Chapter 8, Handling Typical Build Requirements, explores the features provided by Maven to handle builds of selective sources and the inclusion of selected resources. It also describes how to use the command line and help features of Maven along with interfacing with software configuration management systems.

Chapter 9, Multi-module Projects, describes the support required to build large projects with multiple modules. Maven support for aggregated builds and defining parent-child relationships is also described here.

Chapter 10, Java Development with Maven, describes the building of different types of java artifacts like Jar, War and Ear. It also describes Maven support to run projects in Jetty and Tomcat.

Chapter 11, Advanced Maven Usage, explores the advanced features of Maven, such as creating distributions and enforcing rules. It also describes how to make a project release.

What you need for this book

To run the various recipes in this book, the following are required. Unless otherwise mentioned, it is best to have the latest version of the software suggested here:

- ▸ A computer with one of the three operating systems, such as Microsoft Windows, Mac OS X or Linux, and preferably recent/supported versions
- ▸ Java—specifically Java Development Kit (JDK)
- ▸ Apache Maven
- ▸ Git—for examples related to version control systems
- ▸ One or more of the following IDEs:
    - ❑ Eclipse
    - ❑ NetBeans
    - ❑ IntelliJ IDEA

Who this book is for

Apache Maven Cookbook is intended for those of you who are seeking to learn what build automation is and how Apache Maven can be used for this purpose. It is also meant for you if you're familiar with Maven, but would like to understand the finer nuances of it to solve specific problems. It is also a good book if you're looking for ready-made recipes to solve specific use cases.

Sections

In this book, you will find several headings that appear frequently (Getting ready, How to do it, How it works, There's more, and See also).

To give clear instructions on how to complete a recipe, we use these sections as follows:

Getting ready

This section tells you what to expect in the recipe, and describes how to set up any software or any preliminary settings required for the recipe.

How to do it...

This section contains the steps required to follow the recipe.

How it works...

This section usually consists of a detailed explanation of what happened in the previous section.

There's more...

This section consists of additional information about the recipe in order to make the reader more knowledgeable about the recipe.

See also

This section provides helpful links to other useful information for the recipe.

Conventions

In this book, you will find a number of text styles that distinguish between different kinds of information. Here are some examples of these styles and an explanation of their meaning.

Code words in text, database table names, folder names, filenames, file extensions, pathnames, dummy URLs, user input, and Twitter handles are shown as follows: "The preceding output will still not tell you where your Java is installed, which is required to set JAVA_HOME."

A block of code is set as follows:

```
<reporting>
  <plugins>
    <plugin>
      <artifactId>maven-project-info-reports-plugin</artifactId>
      <version>2.0.1</version>
      <reportSets>
        <reportSet></reportSet>
      </reportSets>
    </plugin>
  </plugins>
</reporting>
```

When we wish to draw your attention to a particular part of a code block, the relevant lines or items are set in bold:

```
<settings xmlns="http://maven.apache.org/SETTINGS/1.0.0"
  xmlns:xsi="http://www.w3.org/2001/XMLSchema-instance"
 xsi:schemaLocation="http://maven.apache.org/SETTINGS/1.0.0
                    http://maven.apache.org/xsd/settings-
1.0.0.xsd">
     <localRepository>C:/software/maven</localRepository>
</settings>
```

Any command-line input or output is written as follows:

```
brew install maven
```

New terms and **important words** are shown in bold. Words that you see on the screen, for example, in menus or dialog boxes, appear in the text like this: "To persist this, set **Environment Variables...** using the **Control Panel** option, as described later for the M2_HOME variable."

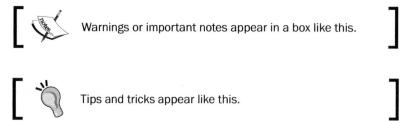

Warnings or important notes appear in a box like this.

Tips and tricks appear like this.

Reader feedback

Feedback from our readers is always welcome. Let us know what you think about this book—what you liked or disliked. Reader feedback is important for us as it helps us develop titles that you will really get the most out of.

To send us general feedback, simply e-mail `feedback@packtpub.com`, and mention the book's title in the subject of your message.

If there is a topic that you have expertise in and you are interested in either writing or contributing to a book, see our author guide at `www.packtpub.com/authors`.

Customer support

Now that you are the proud owner of a Packt book, we have a number of things to help you to get the most from your purchase.

Downloading the example code

You can download the example code files from your account at `http://www.packtpub.com` for all the Packt Publishing books you have purchased. If you purchased this book elsewhere, you can visit `http://www.packtpub.com/support` and register to have the files e-mailed directly to you.

Downloading the color images of this book

We also provide you with a PDF file that has color images of the screenshots/diagrams used in this book. The color images will help you better understand the changes in the output. You can download this file from `https://www.packtpub.com/sites/default/files/downloads/ApacheMavenCookbook_ColorImages.pdf`.

Errata

Although we have taken every care to ensure the accuracy of our content, mistakes do happen. If you find a mistake in one of our books—maybe a mistake in the text or the code—we would be grateful if you could report this to us. By doing so, you can save other readers from frustration and help us improve subsequent versions of this book. If you find any errata, please report them by visiting `http://www.packtpub.com/submit-errata`, selecting your book, clicking on the **Errata Submission Form** link, and entering the details of your errata. Once your errata are verified, your submission will be accepted and the errata will be uploaded to our website or added to any list of existing errata under the Errata section of that title.

To view the previously submitted errata, go to `https://www.packtpub.com/books/content/support` and enter the name of the book in the search field. The required information will appear under the **Errata** section.

Piracy

Piracy of copyrighted material on the Internet is an ongoing problem across all media. At Packt, we take the protection of our copyright and licenses very seriously. If you come across any illegal copies of our works in any form on the Internet, please provide us with the location address or website name immediately so that we can pursue a remedy.

Please contact us at `copyright@packtpub.com` with a link to the suspected pirated material.

We appreciate your help in protecting our authors and our ability to bring you valuable content.

Questions

If you have a problem with any aspect of this book, you can contact us at `questions@packtpub.com`, and we will do our best to address the problem.

1
Getting Started

In this chapter, we will cover the basic tasks related to getting started with Apache Maven:

- ▶ Installing Maven on Microsoft Windows
- ▶ Installing Maven on Mac OS X
- ▶ Installing Maven on Linux
- ▶ Changing the JDK used by Maven
- ▶ Creating a simple project with Maven
- ▶ Building a simple project with Maven
- ▶ Changing the location of the Maven repository
- ▶ Running Maven behind an HTTP proxy server
- ▶ Understanding the standard directory layout

Introduction

Apache Maven is a popular tool for build automation, primarily Java projects. Maven addresses two aspects of building software. First, it describes how a software is built and, second, it describes its dependencies. It uses conventions for the build procedure. An XML file describes the software project being built, its dependencies on other external modules and components, the build order, directories, and required plugins. It comes with predefined targets to perform certain well-defined tasks, such as code compilation and its packaging. Maven dynamically downloads Java libraries and Maven plugins from one or more repositories, such as the **Maven Central Repository**, and stores them locally.

Ever since Maven 1.0 was released in 2004, it has gained popularity and is today the build tool for a large number of open source and commercial projects.

If you are reading this book, then you are not here to understand why Maven is required. You are here to explore Maven and unleash the potential that it offers. The objective of this book is to make the reader aware of Maven's various features, which include installation, configuration, and simple to complex usage by means of examples, illustrations, and working projects.

A brief comparison with other build automation tools

Let's briefly discuss some build automation tools:

> ▸ **Make**: If you are from the C programming world, chances are you have used Make. Makefiles are not platform-independent. They are not natively compatible with Windows. Thus, they are unsuited to build Java projects.

> ▸ **Ant**: This is modeled after Make and has targets and dependencies. Each target has a set of tasks. Ant doesn't have any conventions. It is procedural and does not have the concept of a build lifecycle. Maven has conventions, is declarative, and has a lifecycle.

In this chapter, we will cover the basics of Maven—installing the software, verifying the installation, and creating, implementing, and building a simple Java project. We will also cover a few advanced items, such as changing the location of the repository or running Maven behind an HTTP proxy server as it could be relevant to those who have issues with the way Maven works by default.

Let us start by setting up Maven. We will cover how to do this on the three popular operating systems, namely Microsoft Windows, Mac OS X, and Linux.

Installing Maven on Microsoft Windows

At the time of writing this book, Microsoft Windows 8.1 is the latest version of Microsoft Windows. While the screenshots and output will be for Microsoft Windows 8.1, the steps are similar for earlier (and possibly later) versions as well.

Getting ready

As Maven requires a Java platform, first ensure that you have installed the Java environment on your system, **Java Development Kit** (**JDK**) specifically; **Java Runtime Environment** (**JRE**) is not sufficient.

You can verify whether Java is installed on your system by opening **Add or Remove Programs**. If you see something similar to the following screenshot, JDK is installed on your system:

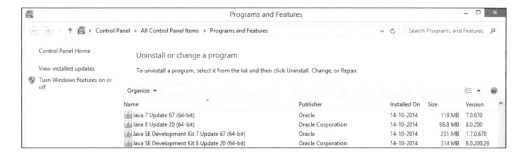

You can also verify the program folder structure from Microsoft Windows Explorer:

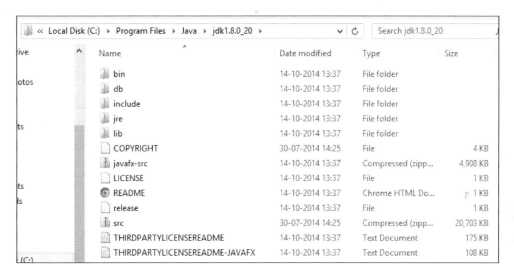

How to do it...

Let's start installing Java and Maven by performing the following steps:

1. Set the variable JAVA_HOME to point to the Java installation that you want Maven to use; for example, you can do this by setting JAVA_HOME variable in the following way:

```
C:\projects\apache_maven_cookbook>set JAVA_HOME=C:\Program Files\
Java\jdk1.8.0_20
```

Note that this setting will not be persisted once the command prompt is closed. To persist this, set **Environment Variables...** using the **Control Panel** option, as described later for the `M2_HOME` variable.

2. If JDK is not installed on your system, now is the time to download and install it from the Oracle Java SE download page at `http://www.oracle.com/technetwork/java/javase/downloads/index.html`.

    Once it is installed, ensure `JAVA_HOME` is set as described earlier.

    Now that we have set up Java, let us download and set up Maven.

3. Go to `http://maven.apache.org/` and click on the **Download** link.

4. The links to the latest stable versions of Maven are displayed.

5. The binaries are available in both, `.zip` and `.tar.gz` formats. Choose one of them.

6. Extract the downloaded binary to a folder you want Maven to reside in. In this case I have chosen `C:\software`.

 It is best to avoid folders with spaces as some features of Maven or its plugins might not work.

7. Ensure the contents are similar to the following screenshot:

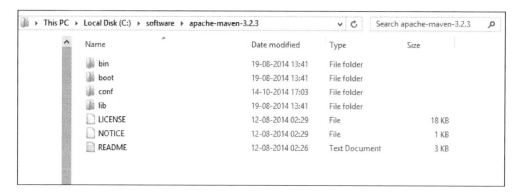

The preceding screenshot displays a list of directories contained in Maven.

Now let's briefly discuss what these directories contain:

- The `bin` folder contains the batch files and shell scripts to run Maven on various platforms.

- The `boot` folder contains the jars required for Maven to start.

- The `conf` folder contains the default `settings.xml` file used by Maven.

- The `lib` folder contains the libraries used by Maven. It also contains an `ext` folder in which third-party extensions, which can extend or override the default Maven implementation, can be placed.

Now let us make sure we can run Maven from the command prompt by carrying out the following steps:

1. Open **Control Panel**:

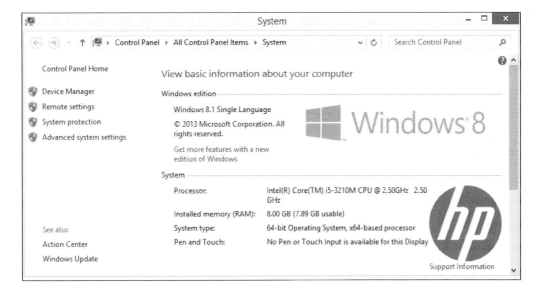

2. Choose **Advanced system settings**:

3. Click on **Environment Variables...**. Add the M2_HOME variable and set it to the folder where Maven was extracted.

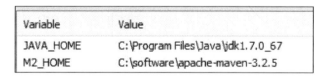

Variable	Value
JAVA_HOME	C:\Program Files\Java\jdk1.7.0_67
M2_HOME	C:\software\apache-maven-3.2.5

4. Edit the PATH variable to include Maven's bin folder:

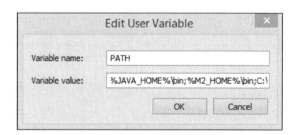

How it works...

A Maven installation is essentially a set of JAR files, configuration files, and a Microsoft Windows batch file, mvn.bat.

The mvn command essentially runs this batch file. It first checks for JAVA_HOME. This file is present in the bin folder of the Maven installation and, hence, it needs to be in PATH.

If the batch file does not find JAVA_HOME, it looks for Java in its PATH. This can lead to unexpected results, as typically the Java in PATH is usually the JRE and not the JDK.

The batch file then looks for M2_HOME, which is the location of the Maven installation. It does this so that it can load the libraries that are present.

Additionally, it also reads values specified in MAVEN_OPTS. This variable allows you to run Maven with an additional heap size and other Java parameters.

Using the values for JAVA_HOME, M2_HOME, and Maven_OPTS, the batch file runs its main class org.codehaus.plexus.classworlds.launcher.Launcher.

There's more...

Verify your Maven installation using the following steps:

1. Open a command prompt in Microsoft Windows and run the following command:

   C:\software\apache-maven-cookbook>mvn -version

2. The following output should be displayed:

   ```
   Apache Maven 3.2.5 (12a6b3acb947671f09b81f49094c53f426d8cea1;
   2014-12-14T22:59:23+05:30)
   Maven home: C:\software\apache-maven-3.2.5
   Java version: 1.7.0_67, vendor: Oracle Corporation
   Java home: C:\Program Files\Java\jdk1.7.0_67\jre
   Default locale: en_IN, platform encoding: Cp1252
   ```
   OS name: "windows 8.1", version: "6.3", arch: "amd64", family: "windows"

See also

▶ The *Creating a simple project with Maven* recipe in this chapter

Installing Maven on Mac OS X

Let us look at the steps to install Maven on Mac OS X. This applies to the latest version of Mac OS X, namely Yosemite.

Earlier, Apple provided Java for Mac, but stopped doing so from Java 7 onwards. Apple Java is not available on recent versions of Mac OS X.

Getting ready

Let us check if the Java environment is available on your Mac:

1. Open the terminal and run the following command:

   ```
   /usr/libexec/java_home -v 1.7
   ```

2. See if you get an output similar to the following:

   ```
   /Library/Java/JavaVirtualMachines/jdk1.7.0_71.jdk/Contents/
   Home
   ```

3. Run the following command to check if you have Java 8:

   ```
   /usr/libexec/java_home -v 1.8
   ```

4. This should give the following output if Java exists:

   ```
   /Library/Java/JavaVirtualMachines/jdk1.8.0_25.jdk/Contents/Home
   ```

   As you can see, my system has both Java 1.7 and 1.8.

5. Set JAVA_HOME to the desired JDK. This can be done in two ways, depending on what you desire:

   If this is for the duration of the session, run the following command:

   ```
   export
   JAVA_HOME=/Library/Java/JavaVirtualMachines/jdk1.8.0_25.jdk
   /Contents/Home
   ```

   If this is permanent, add the preceding line in .bash_profile in your HOME folder

 Ensure you have the JDK installation and not JRE.

If Java is not present, download and install Java from the Oracle Java download page at http://www.oracle.com/technetwork/java/javase/downloads/index.html.

Once installed, verify the Java installation by following the preceding steps.

Now, let us set up Maven on Mac OS X.

How to do it...

Let's download Maven from its official website by performing the following steps:

1. Go to http://maven.apache.org/ and click on the **Download** link. Links to the latest stable versions of Maven will be displayed.

2. The binaries are available in both .zip and .tar.gz formats. Choose one of them.

3. Extract the downloaded binary to the folder you want Maven to reside in. The typical location for the Mac is /usr/local folder.

4. You will need a super user (su) or administrator access to place the contents in the /usr/local folder. If you do not have access, you can place the contents in a subfolder of your HOME folder.

5. Ensure the contents are similar to the following output by executing the following command:

    ```
    /usr/local/apache-maven-3.2.5$ ls -l
    ```

    The output is shown as:

    ```
    total 27
    -rw-r--r--     1 root     wheel     17464 Aug 12 02:29 LICENSE
    -rw-r--r--     1 root     wheel       182 Aug 12 02:29 NOTICE
    -rw-r--r--     1 root     wheel      2508 Aug 12 02:26 README.txt
    drwxr-xr-x     8 root     wheel      4096 Aug 19 13:41 bin
    drwxr-xr-x     3 root     wheel         0 Aug 19 13:41 boot
    drwxr-xr-x     4 root     wheel         0 Oct 14 17:39 conf
    drwxr-xr-x    67 root     wheel     28672 Aug 19 13:41 lib
    ```

6. Set the M2_HOME variable as follows:

    ```
    export M2_HOME=/usr/local/apache-maven-3.2.5
    ```

7. Update the PATH to include Maven's bin folder:

    ```
    export PATH=$PATH:$M2_HOME/bin
    ```

 Like JAVA_HOME, the preceding settings can be persisted by updating .bash_profile with the preceding lines.

In the preceding steps, we discussed the steps to download Maven from its official website. We will now discuss installing Maven using brew. Brew is a popular application on Mac OS X to install open source software. If you have brew installed on your Mac OS X, run the following command to install Maven:

```
brew install maven
```

The output for the preceding command will be displayed as shown in the following screenshot:

```
● ● ●                      Documents — bash — 80×24
MacBook-Pro:~ raghu$ brew install maven
==> Downloading http://www.apache.org/dyn/closer.cgi?path=maven/maven-3/3.2.5/bi
==> Best Mirror http://apache.bytenet.in/maven/maven-3/3.2.5/binaries/apache-mav
################################################################### 100.0%
🍺 /usr/local/Cellar/maven/3.2.5: 82 files, 9.1M, built in 6 seconds
```

How it works...

The Maven installation is essentially a set of JAR files, configuration files, and a Mac OS X shell script, namely mvn.

The mvn command essentially runs this script. It first checks for JAVA_HOME. This file is present in the bin folder of the Maven installation and, hence, it needs to be in PATH.

If the shell script does not find JAVA_HOME, it looks for Java in its PATH. This can lead to unexpected results, as typically the Java in PATH is usually the JRE installation and not JDK.

The shell script then looks for M2_HOME, which is the location for the Maven installation. It does this so that it can load the libraries that are present.

Additionally, it also reads values specified in MAVEN_OPTS. This variable allows you to run Maven with an additional heap size and other Java parameters.

Using the values for JAVA_HOME, M2_HOME, and MAVEN_OPTS, the shell script runs its main class org.codehaus.plexus.classworlds.launcher.Launcher.

There's more...

Verify your Maven installation using the following steps:

1. Open a command prompt and run the following command:

    ```
    mvn -version
    ```

2. The output for the preceding command should be displayed as shown in the following screenshot:

```
● ● ●                    Documents — bash — 80×24
MacBook-Pro:~ raghu$ mvn -version
Apache Maven 3.2.5 (12a6b3acb947671f09b81f49094c53f426d8cea1; 2014-12-14T22:59:2
3+05:30)
Maven home: /usr/local/Cellar/maven/3.2.5/libexec
Java version: 1.8.0_25, vendor: Oracle Corporation
Java home: /Library/Java/JavaVirtualMachines/jdk1.8.0_25.jdk/Contents/Home/jre
Default locale: en_US, platform encoding: UTF-8
OS name: "mac os x", version: "10.10.2", arch: "x86_64", family: "mac"
```

See also

▸ The *Creating a simple project with Maven* recipe in this chapter

Installing Maven on Linux

Let us look at the steps to install Maven on Linux.

While there are many flavors of Linux (Ubuntu, Fedora, RHEL, SUSE, CentOS, and so on), the steps to set up Maven are similar.

Getting ready

Maven needs Java, specifically the Java Development Kit (JDK). Using the following steps, let us check if it is installed in your Linux system, which is a bit tricky:

1. Open a terminal and run the following command:

   java -version

2. See if you get an output similar to the following:

   java version "1.7.0_65"

   OpenJDK Runtime Environment (rhel-2.5.1.2.el6_5-x86_64 u65-b17)

   The preceding output will still not tell you where your Java is installed, which is required to set JAVA_HOME. You can get this information by performing the next set of steps.

3. Check if javac works; it does only if JDK is installed, not JRE:

   $ javac -version

   The output for the preceding command is shown as:

   javac 1.7.0_65

4. Find the location of the `javac` command:

   ```
   $ which javac
   ```

   The output for the preceding command is shown as:

   ```
   /usr/bin/javac
   ```

5. In the preceding output, `javac` is a symbolic link to the actual location of the file. Try to determine this location in the following way:

   ```
   $ readlink /usr/bin/javac
   ```

   The output for the preceding command is shown as:

   ```
   /etc/alternatives/javac
   ```

6. By executing the preceding command, we again got the symbolic link. To get the path to the location of `javac`, we execute the following command again:

   ```
   $ readlink /etc/alternatives/javac
   ```

   The output for the preceding command is shown as:

   ```
   /usr/lib/jvm/java-1.7.0-openjdk.x86_64/bin/javac
   ```

7. We have now located the folder where JDK is installed:

   ```
   /usr/lib/jvm/java-1.7.0-openjdk.x86_64/
   ```

8. Set `JAVA_HOME` to the preceding folder. This can be done in two ways, depending on what you desire:

   If it is for the duration of the session, run the following command:

   ```
   export JAVA_HOME=/usr/lib/jvm/java-1.7.0-openjdk.x86_64/
   ```

   If this is permanent, add the preceding line in `.bash_profile` in your HOME folder.

If Java is not present, download and install Java from the Oracle Java download page at `http://www.oracle.com/technetwork/java/javase/downloads/index.html`.

If you have an rpm-based Linux distribution, you can download and install `rpm`. Otherwise, you can download the `.tar.gz` format of the distribution and extract it to a folder of your choice.

In the earlier case, you know exactly where Java is installed and can set `JAVA_HOME` correspondingly. Once installed, verify the Java installation by following the preceding steps.

Now, let us set up Maven on Linux.

How to do it...

To set up Maven on Linux, perform the following steps:

1. Go to `http://maven.apache.org/` and click on the **Download** link. The links to latest stable versions of Maven will be displayed.

2. The binaries are available in both `.zip` and `.tar.gz` formats. For Mac OS X and Linux, the preferred download format is `.tar.gz`.

3. Extract the downloaded binary to a folder you want Maven to reside in. The typical location in Linux is the `/usr/local` folder.

> You will need a super user (su) or administrator access to place contents in the `/usr/local` folder. If you do not have access, you can place this in a subfolder of your HOME folder.

4. Execute the following command, and ensure the contents of the `apache-maven-3.2.5` folder are similar to the following output:

   `/usr/local/apache-maven-3.2.5$ ls -l`

   The output for the preceding command is shown as:

   ```
   total 27
   -rw-r--r--    1 root      root      17464 Aug 12 02:29 LICENSE
   -rw-r--r--    1 root      root        182 Aug 12 02:29 NOTICE
   -rw-r--r--    1 root      root       2508 Aug 12 02:26 README.txt
   drwxr-xr-x    8 root      root       4096 Aug 19 13:41 bin
   drwxr-xr-x    3 root      root          0 Aug 19 13:41 boot
   drwxr-xr-x    4 root      root          0 Oct 14 17:39 conf
   drwxr-xr-x   67 root      root      28672 Aug 19 13:41 lib
   ```

5. Set the M2_HOME variable as follows:

   `export M2_HOME=/usr/local/apache-maven-3.2.5`

6. Update PATH to include Maven's `bin` folder:

   `export PATH=$PATH:$M2_HOME/bin`

Like JAVA_HOME, the preceding settings can be persisted by updating `.bash_profile`.

How it works...

The Maven installation is essentially a set of JAR files, configuration files, and a Linux shell script, namely `mvn`.

The `mvn` command essentially runs this script. It first checks for `JAVA_HOME`. This file is present in the `bin` folder of the Maven installation and hence needs to be in `PATH`.

If the shell script does not find `JAVA_HOME`, it looks for `java` in its `PATH`. This can lead to unexpected results, as typically, the `Java` in `PATH` is usually JRE and not JDK.

The shell script then looks for `M2_HOME`, which is the location of the Maven installation. It does this so that it can load the libraries that are present.

Additionally, it also reads values specified in `MAVEN_OPTS`. This variable allows you to run Maven with an additional heap size and other Java parameters.

Using the values for `JAVA_HOME`, `M2_HOME`, and `MAVEN_OPTS`, the shell script runs its `org.codehaus.plexus.classworlds.launcher.Launcher` main class.

There's more...

Using the following steps, let's confirm that Maven has been set up correctly, by running a Maven command:

1. Open a command prompt and run the following command:

   `mvn -version`

2. The following output should be displayed:

   ```
   Apache Maven 3.2.5
   (12a6b3acb947671f09b81f49094c53f426d8cea1; 2014-12-
   14T22:59:23+05:30)
   ```

   ```
   Maven home: /usr/local/maven
   ```

   ```
   Java version: 1.7.0_65, vendor: Oracle Corporation
   ```

   ```
   Java home: /usr/lib/jvm/java-1.7.0-openjdk-
   1.7.0.65.x86_64/jre
   ```

   ```
   Default locale: en_US, platform encoding: ANSI_X3.4-1968
   ```

   `OS name: "linux", version: "2.6.32-279.22.1.el6.x86_64",`
   `arch: "amd64", family: "unix"`

If you get an error, recheck the installation steps and repeat them.

See also

▶ The *Creating a simple project with Maven* recipe in this chapter

Changing the JDK used by Maven

It is possible to have more than one version of JDK installed on your system. By following some simple steps, you can specify and/or change the JDK to be used by Maven.

How to do it...

You will recall that, in the earlier section, we used Java SE 7. Let us now change to Java SE 8. To change the JDK version to Java SE 8 on Microsoft Windows, perform the following steps:

1. From the command prompt, run the following command:

   ```
   set JAVA_HOME=C:\Program Files\Java\jdk1.8.0_20
   ```

2. For Linux or Mac, the command will be:

   ```
   export JAVA_HOME=<java-8-home-folder>
   ```

3. Now, run the following command to check the version of Maven installed:

   ```
   mvn -version
   ```

4. To check the version of Maven installed on Microsoft Windows, run the following command from the command prompt. You should get the following output. The output will be similar for Linux and Mac:

   ```
   C:\projects\apache-maven-cookbook>mvn -version
   ```

   The output for the preceding command is shown as:

   ```
   Apache Maven 3.2.5
   (12a6b3acb947671f09b81f49094c53f426d8cea1; 2014-12-
   14T22:59:23+05:30)
   Maven home: C:\software\apache-maven-3.2.5
   Java version: 1.8.0_20, vendor: Oracle Corporation
   Java home: C:\Program Files\Java\jdk1.8.0_20\jre
   Default locale: en_IN, platform encoding: Cp1252
   OS name: "windows 8.1", version: "6.3", arch: "amd64", family:
   "windows"
   ```

How it works...

Maven always uses the JDK specified by JAVA_HOME, no matter how many JDK installations are available on the system. This allows the user the flexibility to change JDKs as required or based on the project.

Hence, it is important to ensure JAVA_HOME is defined. In the absence of this variable, Maven attempts to detect the presence of Java from PATH. This is typically JRE and not JDK.

Creating a simple project with Maven

Now that we have set up Maven on our favorite operating system and verified that it works fine, it is time to create a simple Java project.

Maven makes it easy to bootstrap a new project by creating a bunch of files and folders following accepted conventions.

How to do it...

Let's start creating the first simple project using Maven, by performing the following steps:

1. Open a command prompt and change the directory to the folder in which you want to create your first Maven project.

2. Run the following command:

    ```
    mvn archetype:generate -DgroupId=com.packt.cookbook -
    DartifactId=simple-project -DarchetypeArtifactId=maven-
    archetype-quickstart -DinteractiveMode=false
    ```

    You can change the groupId and artifactId values in the preceding command as per your requirement.

3. You will see Maven downloading a bunch of files:

    ```
    Downloading:
    https://repo.maven.apache.org/maven2/org/apache/maven/plugi
    ns/maven-clean-plugin/2.5/maven-clean-plugin-2.5.pom
    ```

    ```
    Downloaded:
    https://repo.maven.apache.org/maven2/org/apache/maven/plugi
    ns/maven-clean-plugin/2.5/maven-clean-plugin-2.5.pom (4 KB
    at 1.4 KB/sec)
    ```

4. Then it will start generating sources:

    ```
    [INFO] >>> maven-archetype-plugin:2.2:generate (default-
    cli) > generate-sources
    ```

    ```
    @ standalone-pom >>>
    ```

5. When Maven has completed generating sources, it will create the project that we want:

```
[INFO] Using following parameters for creating project from
Old (1.x) Archetype:
maven-archetype-quickstart:1.0
[INFO] ----------------------------------------------------
-----------------------
[INFO] Parameter: groupId, Value: com.packt.cookbook
[INFO] Parameter: packageName, Value: com.packt.cookbook
[INFO] Parameter: package, Value: com.packt.cookbook
[INFO] Parameter: artifactId, Value: simple-project
[INFO] Parameter: basedir, Value: C:\projects\apache-maven-
cookbook
[INFO] Parameter: version, Value: 1.0-SNAPSHOT
[INFO] project created from Old (1.x) Archetype in dir:
C:\projects\apache-maven-cookbook\simple-project
```

Downloading the example code

You can download the example code files from your account at http://www.packtpub.com for all the Packt Publishing books you have purchased. If you purchased this book elsewhere, you can visit http://www.packtpub.com/support and register to have the files e-mailed directly to you.

How it works...

Did you get an while error running the preceding command to create your simple project?

One possibility is that your Maven is behind an HTTP proxy server. If so, see the *Running Maven behind an HTTP proxy server* recipe in this chapter.

Let's look at the folder structure that is created:

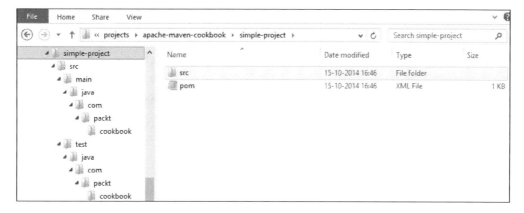

You will notice the following things:

▸ The Maven project configuration file `pom.xml` is created in the root of the `simple-project` folder. We will explore this file in detail in subsequent sections.

▸ A bunch of folders are created:

   ❏ `src\main\java`: This is for Java source files

   ❏ `src\test\java`: This is for Java test source files

   ❏ `src\main\resources`: This is for resource files for the project

   ❏ `src\test\resources`: This is for resource files for the test

▸ Within each of the preceding folders, a folder structure corresponding to the `groupId` (`org.packt.cookbook`) is created.

The following are essentially Maven conventions at work:

▸ Maven expects all Java source files to reside in `src\main\java`

▸ Similarly, it expects all Java test files to reside in `src\test\java`

▸ It expects all project resources to reside in `src\main\resources` and test resources to reside in `src\test\resources`

▸ It expects that source files will typically have the same package structure as the `groupId` parameter (though this is not mandatory)

▸ Two sample classes, namely `App.java` and `AppTest.java`, are also created and it is not expected that they will be used beyond testing how Maven works

The `mvn` command that we used in the *Creating a simple project with Maven* recipe in this chapter, tries to invoke the `generate` goal of the `archetype` plugin with the specified command-line parameters.

The default Maven installation has minimal features. All features of Maven are available as Maven plugins. When given a plugin name, Maven knows where to download it from and then run it.

In this case, Maven downloads the `archetype` plugin. This plugin, in turn, can depend on another plugin. In this case, the latter plugin gets downloaded. This happens in a recursive fashion and, at the end of the process, all the relevant plugins required to run the specified command are downloaded.

These plugins are placed in your local repository, which is a location in your system. Once downloaded, these are never downloaded again unless deleted.

▶ The *Running Maven behind an HTTP proxy server* recipe in this chapter

Building a simple project with Maven

Let us now build the project that was created in the preceding section.

How to do it...

To build the previously created simple project with Maven, perform the following steps:

1. Open the command prompt and run the following command, changing the directory to the folder the project was created:

    ```
    mvn package
    ```

2. Observe the following things in the output:

    Notice the following warning (we will see how to resolve this later in this book):

    ```
    [INFO] --- maven-resources-plugin:2.6:resources (default-
    resources) @ simple-project ---
    ```

    [WARNING] Using platform encoding (Cp1252 actually) to copy
    filtered resources,

    i.e. build is platform dependent!

    Check if the sources are compiled:

    ```
    [INFO] --- maven-compiler-plugin:3.1:compile (default-
    compile) @ simple-project
    ```

    Check if the tests are run:

    ```
    [INFO] --- maven-surefire-plugin:2.12.4:test (default-test)
    @ simple-project ---

    [INFO] Surefire report directory: C:\projects\apache-maven-
    cookbook\simple-project\target\surefire-reports

    -------------------------------------------------------

     T E S T S

    -------------------------------------------------------

    Running com.packt.cookbook.AppTest
    ```
    Tests run: 1, Failures: 0, Errors: 0, Skipped: 0, Time
    elapsed: 0.005 sec

3. A JAR file is now created.

How it works...

In the `mvn package` command, the `package` parameter is a phase in the build lifecycle. Maven has a default build lifecycle that has a number of phases. Each phase will execute every phase prior to it in order along with the specified phase. In this case, the `package` phase executes in the following order:

▸ Validate

▸ Compile

▸ Test

▸ Package

The `validate` phase makes sure that the project (specifically the `pom.xml` file that describes the project) is in order and all the necessary information to run the project is available.

The `compile` phase compiles the sources.

The `test` phase compiles the test sources and then runs the test using a suitable test framework. In the earlier example, the **JUnit** framework is used to run the tests.

The `package` phase packages the artifacts to the format specified in the `pom.xml` file.

Changing the location of the Maven repository

There are three types of Maven repositories:

▸ **Local**: This is the repository in your computer filesystem

▸ **Remote**: This is the repository from where the required Maven files get downloaded

▸ **Mirrors**: These are repository managers, such as **Nexus** and **Artifactory**, that mirror various repositories

You will have seen Maven downloading a number of files (called poms and jars). Let us see where they are located in your computer:

▸ Go to your HOME folder (`C:\Users\username`) in the case of Microsoft Windows, `/Users/username` for Mac, and, `/home/username` (or a similar location) for Linux

▸ You will notice the `.m2` folder and within that, a subfolder called `repository`

 Any folder that starts with a dot (.) is typically hidden from view. You will need to change your folder viewer settings to see it.

▸ You will see a number of folders and files that are used by Maven

You may want to change this location for the following reasons:

▸ You may want to conserve space in the C drive and store these folders and files in the D drive on Microsoft Windows.

▸ You may want to take a back up of the contents. Backup software usually backs up contents in specific folders of the filesystem.

▸ Your organization may have a policy for all users to store a local repository in the same folder.

How to do it...

To change the location of the Maven repository, perform the following steps:

1. Create a file called `settings.xml` in the `.m2` folder.

2. Add the following contents to the settings.xml file that you just created:

```
<settings xmlns="http://maven.apache.org/SETTINGS/1.0.0"
   xmlns:xsi="http://www.w3.org/2001/XMLSchema-instance"
  xsi:schemaLocation="http://maven.apache.org/SETTINGS/1.0.0
                      http://maven.apache.org/xsd/settings-
1.0.0.xsd">
      <localRepository>C:/software/maven</localRepository>
</settings>
```

Notice the highlighted part of the preceding code. We have changed the location of the repository contents to C:\software\maven. You can change it to any valid folder name.

3. Delete the `repository` subfolder and run the `mvn package` command again.

You will now notice that the `repository` folder is not created in the `.m2` folder. Instead, it is created in `C:\software\maven`.

How it works...

Maven determines the location of the local repository in the following way:

▸ If `settings.xml` exists in the user's `.m2` folder, which contains the `<localRepository>` tag, then Maven uses its contents to determine the location

▸ If not, Maven will check if `localRepository` is explicitly defined in the default `settings.xml`, present in the `conf` folder of the Maven installation

▸ If it is not present there, Maven will use the default value for the local repository, which is the user's `.m2` folder

Running Maven behind an HTTP proxy server

Most organizations do not allow devices in their network to access the Internet directly for security and other reasons. In such cases, typically, a proxy server comes into picture. The proxy server details are specified in the browser or any other location where access to the Internet is required.

How to do it...

Let's start running Maven behind an HTTP proxy server, by performing the following steps:

1. Create a `settings.xml` file in the `.m2` folder in your HOME directory, if it does not exist already.

2. Add the following code within the `settings` tag:

    ```
    <proxies>
      <proxy>
        <id>myproxy</id>
        <active>true</active>
        <protocol>http</protocol>
        <host>proxy.myorg.com</host>
        <port>8080</port>
        <username>proxyuser</username>
        <password>somepassword</password>
        <nonProxyHosts>*.myorg.com </nonProxyHosts>
      </proxy>
    </proxies>
    ```

If the proxy server does not need authentication, the `username` and `password` tags can be omitted.

The `nonProxyHosts` tag allows you to specify locations that can be accessed directly (for instance, your intranet). This can be skipped if not relevant.

How it works...

Maven needs Internet access to download plugins and dependencies. When Maven runs, it reads the user's `settings.xml` file, if it exists. It checks for any active proxy settings and applies the same.

Maven uses the values in the proxy settings to download any artifacts from the repository. If there are no artifacts to be downloaded, then these values are not used.

The HTTP proxy server may work only in your organization's network. If you are running Maven from a different network, you may want to turn off the HTTP proxy server. This can be done by setting the `active` tag to `false` in the preceding code.

Understanding the standard directory layout

When we built our sample Java project earlier, we saw files being compiled, tests being run, and a JAR being generated. We do not know where these artifacts were created.

How to do it...

Let's find where the artifacts were created by performing the following steps:

1. Go to the folder that has the sample Maven project.
2. Open the `target` subfolder that was created:

```
Directory of C:\projects\apache-maven-cookbook\simple-project\target
18-10-2014  08:12    <DIR>          .
18-10-2014  08:12    <DIR>          ..
18-10-2014  08:12    <DIR>          classes
18-10-2014  08:12    <DIR>          maven-archiver
18-10-2014  08:12    <DIR>          maven-status
18-10-2014  08:12             2,362 simple-project-1.0-SNAPSHOT.jar
18-10-2014  08:12    <DIR>          surefire-reports
18-10-2014  08:12    <DIR>          test-classes
```

How it works...

When Maven runs, it puts all the contents that it generates into a separate folder. This is to distinguish it from any user-generated content. Let us examine the contents of this folder:

- The `classes` folder: Compiled source files are placed in this folder. This folder will also contain resources, such as XML and property files that are part of the source, placed in `src/main/resources`.

- The `test-classes` folder: Compiled test source files are available in this folder. In addition, it also contains test resources, which are files required for the purpose of testing, but not for running the project.

- The `surefire-reports` folder: Test reports are separately placed in this folder. Typically, both XML and HTML report formats are available. The latter can be opened in the browser, while the former can be integrated with a code coverage tool.

- The output `.jar` file: The generated project artifact is also present in this folder.

- Two other folders—`maven-archiver` and `maven-status`—hold information used by Maven during the build.

2

IDE Integration
with Maven

In this chapter, we will see how to set up and use Maven with three popular Java **Integrated Development Environments** (**IDE**). We will cover the following recipes:

- ▶ Creating a new Maven project in Eclipse
- ▶ Importing an existing Maven project in Eclipse
- ▶ Creating a new Maven project in NetBeans
- ▶ Importing an existing Maven project in NetBeans
- ▶ Creating a new Maven project in IntelliJ IDEA
- ▶ Importing an existing Maven project in IntelliJ IDEA

Introduction

IDE improves developer productivity by performing the following functions:

- ▶ Creating boilerplate code
- ▶ Carrying out code completion
- ▶ Identifying syntax issues
- ▶ Performing tasks such as compilation, unit testing, and deploying to web/app servers

While Maven is primarily intended to be a command-line tool, IDEs help developers enjoy as well as exploit Maven features in better ways. The integration of Maven with IDE helps us to automatically download dependencies and quickly search for dependencies through the UI, among other benefits.

The IDE integration of Maven has improved over the years and most Maven features can be set through IDE now.

Creating a new Maven project in Eclipse

Eclipse is one of the most popular open source IDEs. It originated primarily from IBM's VisualAge for Java. It is a platform that allows extensibility by means of plugins (something that Maven does as well). Eclipse can be used to develop not only Java projects, but also a host of other languages by means of plugins.

As of writing this book, Eclipse 4.4.1 (Luna SR1) is the most recent edition. The screenshots in this book are for this version.

Getting ready

Eclipse needs a Java environment to run and hence needs Java to be installed on the system. To do this, refer to the *Getting ready* sections of the first three recipes of *Chapter 1, Getting Started*.

Download Eclipse from `https://www.eclipse.org/downloads/`. Eclipse binaries are available for all popular operating systems. There are also different package solutions of Eclipse targeted at different types of developers (C/C++, Java EE, PHP, and so on). You should choose one of the Eclipse IDEs for Java developers, or the Eclipse IDE for Java EE developers.

> For Maven to work, it is important to start Eclipse using JDK and not JRE. This can be done by passing the following argument to the start up script:
>
> `-vm %JAVA_HOME%\bin\javaw`

The recent versions of Eclipse come preinstalled with Maven support. Let us confirm this by performing the following steps:

1. Launch Eclipse and click on the **About Eclipse** button in the **Help** menu, as shown in the following screenshot:

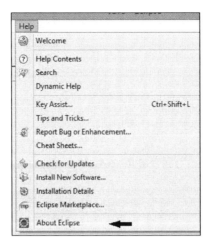

2. Click on the **m2** icon from the list of icons that you see:

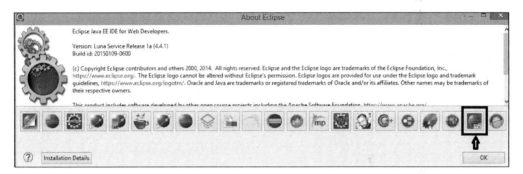

3. On clicking the **m2** icon, you should see something similar to the following screenshot:

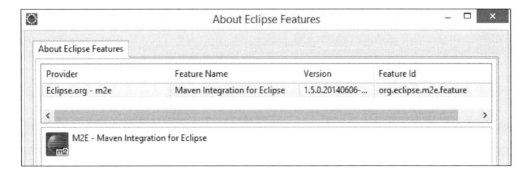

4. Click on the **Maven** link by navigating to **Window | Preferences** from the Eclipse menu bar.

5. Click on **Installations**. You will see the existing installations available to Eclipse. It uses an **EMBEDDED** installation of Maven that comes with Eclipse, as shown in the following screenshot:

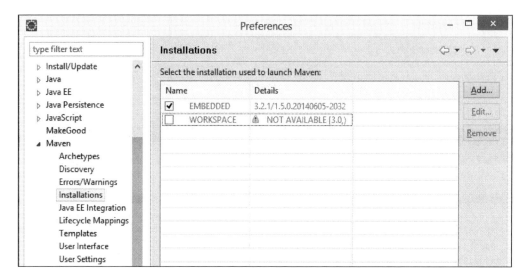

6. Add the Maven installation that you set up by clicking on the **Add...** button.

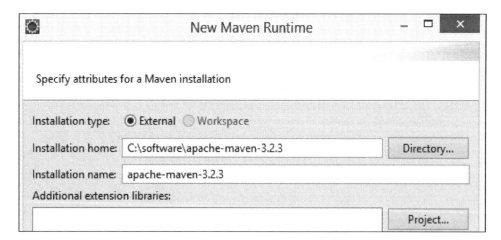

7. You can check this installation so that it is chosen instead of the **EMBEDDED** installation.

How to do it...

To create a new Maven project, perform the following steps:

1. Navigate to **File | New | Maven Project**. You will see the following screen:

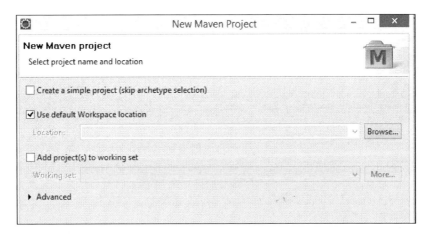

2. Check the **Create a simple project (skip archetype selection)** option to avoid choosing what to create.

3. Fill the same values that we specified as parameters in the *Creating a simple project with Maven* recipe in *Chapter 1, Getting Started* (**Group Id:** com.packt.cookbook, **Artifact Id:** simple-project) to create a simple Maven project.

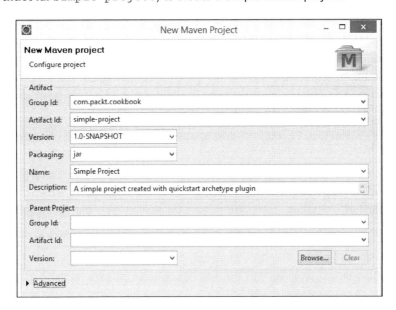

4. Click on **Finish**. Your project is now set up. Click on the `pom.xml` file. You will see the following screenshot:

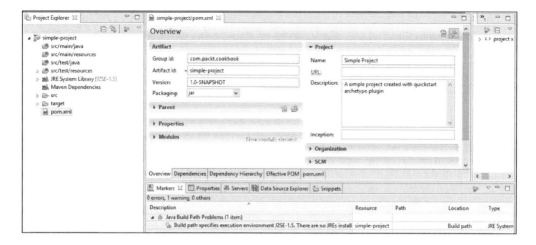

How it works...

Eclipse has built-in support (using the `m2e` plugin) for Maven projects. In this recipe, we used Eclipse to create a simple Maven project, skipping the artifact selection. We also specified the `groupId`, `artifactId`, and `version` for the project.

Using this information, Eclipse invokes the Maven archetype plugin to create a quick start project. The Eclipse console shows the steps performed, and the project is created.

The folder structure and contents are identical to the project created from the command-line.

Importing an existing Maven project in Eclipse

If you have already set up a Maven project from the command-line, then it can easily be imported to Eclipse.

If you have not yet set up Eclipse and verified that Maven exists, please follow the *Getting ready* section of the preceding recipe.

How to do it...

To import an existing Maven project in Eclipse, perform the following steps:

1. Navigate to **File | Import...** and click on **Maven**:

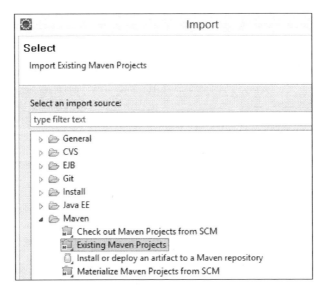

2. Choose the project we created in the previous chapter:

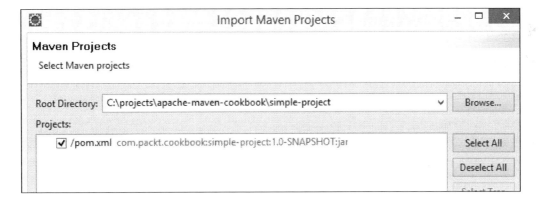

3. Import the project. You will see contents identical to what we saw when creating a new Maven project.

How it works...

Eclipse has built-in support for Maven projects. When a Maven project is imported, it parses the pom file, `pom.xml`, for the specified project. Based on the project's pom configuration file, it creates relevant Eclipse configurations to recognize source files, tests, and artifacts.

It also identifies all the dependencies of the project, downloads these using Maven (if they haven't been downloaded already), and adds them to the project dependencies.

Creating a new Maven project in NetBeans

NetBeans is another popular IDE. This is backed by Oracle, is equally feature-rich and extensible, and supports multiple languages, such as Eclipse.

As of writing this, NetBeans 8.0.2 is the most recent edition. The screenshots in this book reflect this version.

Getting ready

NetBeans can be downloaded in two different ways (if not downloaded already):

▸ Oracle provides a download of the latest JDK along with the latest version of NetBeans. This is a good option, especially if you have not installed JDK yet.

▸ If JDK is already installed, then NetBeans can be downloaded separately from `https://netbeans.org/`. There are different bundles of NetBeans (similar to Eclipse). You can choose one from Java SE or Java EE, or all of them, based on your preference.

How to do it...

Now that NetBeans is installed, let us create a new Maven project, by performing the following steps:

1. Navigate to **Tools | Options**. Choose **Java** and click on the **Maven** tab. You will notice **Maven Home** showing up as **Bundled** with **(Version: 3.0.5)**:

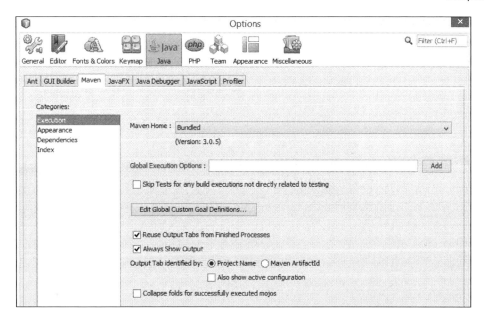

2. You can leave it as is or change it to your Maven installation by choosing the dropdown.

3. Now navigate to **File** | **New Project**.

4. Choose **Maven** from **Categories:** and **Java Application** from **Projects:**, as shown in the following screenshot:

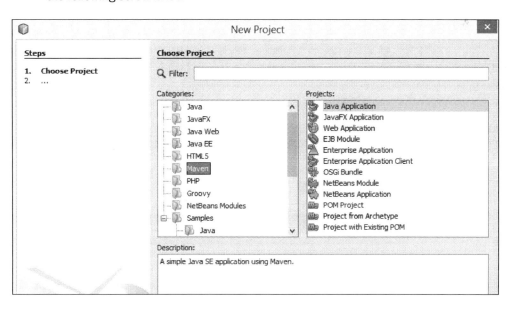

5. Specify the details of the project:

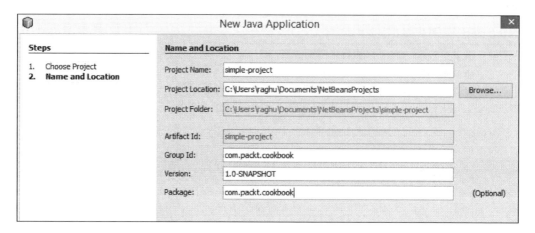

You are done! A new project is now created in NetBeans.

How it works...

Like Eclipse, NetBeans has built-in support for Maven. Unlike Eclipse, NetBeans did not use the Maven archetype for a quick start. Instead, it created a new project using its template. In this case, you will notice that it did not create the dummy source and test class that the quick archetype creates.

Importing an existing Maven project in NetBeans

Instead of creating a new Maven project, as we did in the preceding recipe, you may want to open an existing Maven project in NetBeans. Let us now see how we can import an existing Maven project.

Getting ready

NetBeans can be downloaded in two different ways (if not downloaded already):

- ▸ Oracle provides a download of the latest JDK along with the latest version of NetBeans. This is a good option, especially if you haven't installed JDK yet.

- ▸ If JDK is already installed, then NetBeans can be downloaded separately at `https://netbeans.org/`. There are different bundles of NetBeans (similar to Eclipse). You can choose one from Java SE or Java EE, or all of them, based on your preference.

How to do it...

To import an existing Maven project in NetBeans, perform the following steps:

1. Navigate to **File | Open Project...**:

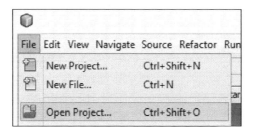

2. Choose the project we created earlier from the command-line. Notice how NetBeans recognizes it (with the **ma** icon) as a Maven project:

3. NetBeans now opens the Maven project.

How it works...

Like Eclipse, NetBeans has built-in support for Maven. It identifies a folder as a Maven project due to the presence of `pom.xml`. It parses this file and opens the project associating the files and folders to **Source Packages**, **Dependencies**, and **Project Files**, as shown in following screenshot:

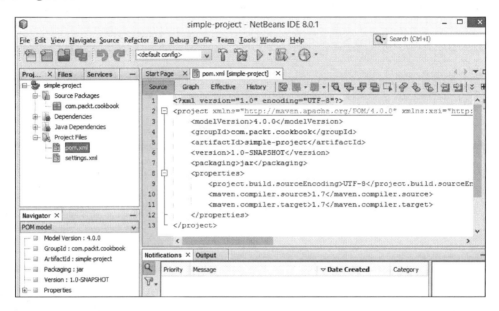

Creating a new Maven project in IntelliJ IDEA

IntelliJ IDEA is an IDE from JetBrains. It has both Community and commercial editions. IntelliJ IDEA is enormously popular among developers and is regularly updated with the latest language and platform features.

For the purpose of this cookbook, we will use the Community Edition. The steps are the same for the commercial edition as well.

As of writing this book, IntelliJ IDEA 14.0.3 is the most recent edition. The screenshots in this book reflect this version.

Getting ready

As IntelliJ IDEA needs a Java environment to run, let us first ensure that the Java environment is set up on our system:

1. Ensure that JDK is installed.

2. Download IntelliJ IDEA by visiting `https://www.jetbrains.com/idea/` and clicking on the **Download** link.

3. Ensure the project SDK is set to your Java installation.

How to do it...

Use the following steps to create a new Maven project in IntelliJ IDEA:

1. Open IntelliJ IDEA.

2. Click on **Create New Project**.

3. Choose **Maven**.

4. Select the **Create from archetype** option and choose **maven-archetype-quickstart:1.1**:

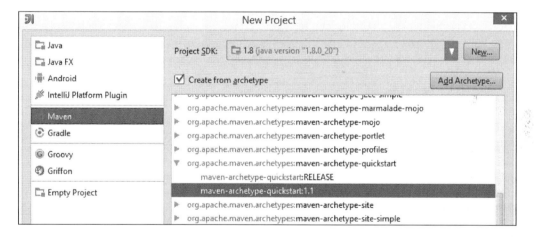

5. Specify the values required to create the project:

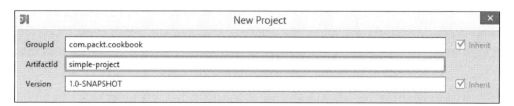

6. Confirm the values for the project:

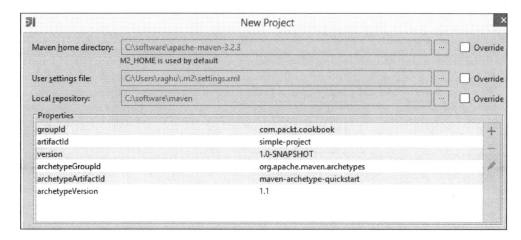

You are done! A new Maven project is created in IntelliJ IDEA.

How it works...

IntelliJ IDEA has first-class support for Maven. It can create a new Maven project as per archetype by downloading the required plugins and dependencies from the repository. It uses the configured Maven settings, which can be customized as specified in the next section.

There's more...

You can customize Maven in IntelliJ IDEA by opening the Maven settings as follows:

1. Navigate to **Configure | Settings**:

2. Click on **Maven** on the left panel:

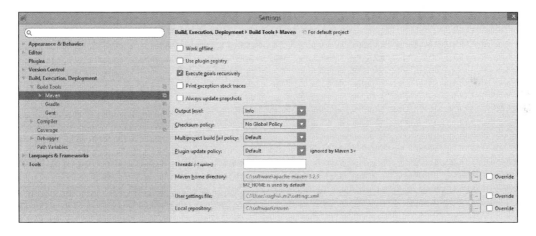

3. Click on **Override** to change the values as you desire.

4. Change a few of the default options such as **Work offline** or **Output level:**, as shown in the preceding screenshot.

Importing an existing Maven project in IntelliJ IDEA

While we can use IntelliJ IDEA to create a new project, in most cases you will already have an existing project in your filesystem. In the latter scenario, you will want to import this project.

Getting ready

As IntelliJ IDEA needs a Java environment to run, let us first ensure that the Java environment is set up on our system:

1. Ensure that JDK is installed.

2. Download IntelliJ IDEA by visiting `https://www.jetbrains.com/idea/` and clicking on the **Download** link.

3. Ensure the project SDK is set to your Java installation.

How to do it...

To import an existing Maven project in IntelliJ IDEA, perform the following steps:

1. Start IntelliJ IDEA.

2. Choose **Import Project**. Browse for the simple project that we created earlier:

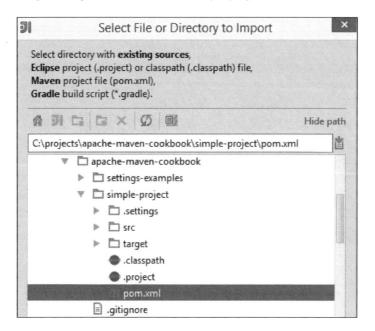

3. Make changes if required. The changes can be made as shown in the following screenshot:

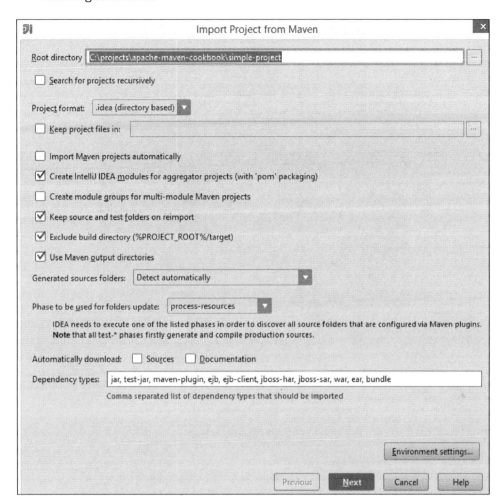

4. Confirm the project to be imported:

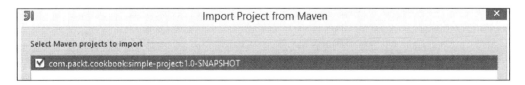

You are done! The existing Maven project is now imported to IntelliJ IDEA.

How it works...

IntelliJ IDEA has first-class support for Maven. It can parse pom files to determine the project structure and dependencies, and lay them out in the IDE.

Once the project is opened in IntelliJ IDEA, the following folders and files get created:

```
C:\projects\apache-maven-cookbook\simple-project>tree /f
Folder PATH listing
Volume serial number is 04B8-E184
C:.
    .classpath
    .project
    pom.xml
    simple-project.iml

    .idea
        .name
        compiler.xml
        encodings.xml
        misc.xml
        modules.xml
        vcs.xml
        workspace.xml

      copyright
          profiles_settings.xml
      libraries
          Maven__junit_junit_3_8_1.xml
      scopes
          scope_settings.xml
```

There's more...

All Maven-related operations can be conducted from the IDE by opening the **Maven Projects** tab in IntelliJ IDEA:

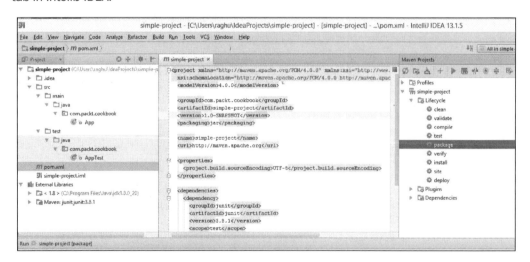

You can choose **Lifecycle** and click on the phase to be run. For instance, in the preceding screenshot, we run the **package** phase of the **Lifecycle**.

3
Maven Lifecycle

Let us start putting Maven to use. In this chapter, we will cover the following recipes:

- ▸ Understanding the Maven lifecycle, phases, and goals
- ▸ Understanding the pom file
- ▸ Understanding Maven settings
- ▸ Understanding command-line options in Maven
- ▸ Understanding Maven profiles
- ▸ Adding a new Maven profile
- ▸ Activating/deactivating a Maven profile
- ▸ Using properties in Maven
- ▸ Specifying source encoding for platform-independent builds

Introduction

We have set up Maven on our computer. We have created a simple Maven project and seen how to build it. We have also set up Maven to run on our preferred IDE.

Let us now understand better how Maven works and how to use it. We will start by understanding the Maven build lifecycle as well as the phases and goals that make up the lifecycle. We will also explore Maven's project configuration pom file as well as the settings file. We will also try to understand what Maven profiles are and why they are needed. Finally, we will look at Maven's properties.

Understanding the Maven lifecycle, phases, and goals

As we start using Maven, we need to understand the Maven project lifecycle. Maven is implemented based around the concept of a build lifecycle. This means there is a clearly defined process to build and distribute artifacts with Maven.

What makes up a lifecycle? The stages of a lifecycle are called phases. In each phase, one or more goals can be executed.

Getting ready

Maven is set up on your system and is verified as working. For setting up Apache Maven, refer to the first three recipes of *Chapter 1, Getting Started*.

How to do it...

To build a Maven project, perform the following steps:

1. Open the command prompt.
2. Run one of the Maven commands that we are familiar with:

   `mvn package`

3. Observe the various steps that get executed.

How it works...

Maven has three built-in build lifecycles:

 ▸ `default`: The `default` lifecycle handles project build and deployment
 ▸ `clean`: The `clean` lifecycle cleans up the files and folders produced by Maven
 ▸ `site`: The `site` lifecycle handles the creation of project documentation

You will have noticed that you do not have to explicitly specify a lifecycle. Instead, what you specify is a phase. Maven infers the lifecycle based on the phase specified.

For instance, the `package` phase indicates it is the `default` lifecycle.

When Maven is run with the `package` phase as a parameter, the `default` build lifecycle gets executed. Maven runs all the phases in sequence, up to and including the specified phase (in our case, the `package` phase).

While each lifecycle has a number of phases, let us look at the important phases for each lifecycle:

- The `clean` lifecycle: The `clean` phase removes all the files and folders created by Maven as part of its build

- The `site` lifecycle: The `site` phase generates the project's documentation, which can be published, as well as a template that can be customized further

- The `default` lifecycle: The following are some of the important phases of the `default` lifecycle:

  - `validate`: This phase validates that all project information is available and correct

  - `process-resources`: This phase copies project resources to the destination to package

  - `compile`: This phase compiles the source code

  - `test`: This phase runs unit tests within a suitable framework

  - `package`: This phase packages the compiled code in its distribution format

  - `integration-test`: This phase processes the package in the integration test environment

  - `verify`: This phase runs checks to verify that the package is valid

  - `install`: This phase installs the package in the local repository

  - `deploy`: This phase installs the final package in the configured repository

Each phase is made up of plugin goals. A plugin goal is a specific task that builds the project. Some goals make sense only in specific phases (for example, the compile goal of the Maven Compiler plugin makes sense in the compile phase, but the `checkstyle` goal of the Maven Checkstyle plugin can potentially be run in any phase). So some goals are bound to a specific phase of a lifecycle, while others are not.

Here is a table of phases, plugins, and goals:

Phase	Plugin	Goal
`clean`	Maven Clean plugin	clean
`site`	Maven Site plugin	site
`process-resources`	Maven Resources plugin	resource
`compile`	Maven Compiler plugin	compile
`test`	Maven Surefire plugin	test
`package`	Varies based on the packaging; for instance, the Maven JAR plugin	jar (in the case of a Maven JAR plugin)

Phase	Plugin	Goal
`install`	Maven Install plugin	install
`deploy`	Maven Deploy plugin	deploy

Understanding the pom file

Every Maven project has a pom file that defines what the project is all about and how it should be built. Pom is an acronym for **project object model**. Let us take a peek at this file.

How to do it...

Let's understand the pom file, by performing the following steps:

1. Go to a Maven project that we created in previous chapters.
2. Open the file named `pom.xml`.

How it works...

A pom file is an XML file that is based on a specific schema, as specified at the top of the file:

```
<project xmlns="http://maven.apache.org/POM/4.0.0"
   xmlns:xsi="http://www.w3.org/2001/XMLSchema-instance"
   xsi:schemaLocation="http://maven.apache.org/POM/4.0.0
                     http://maven.apache.org/xsd/maven-
4.0.0.xsd">
```

There is also a `modelVersion` element that defines the version of this schema:

```
<modelVersion>4.0.0</modelVersion>
```

These are the basic elements of a pom file.

The `groupId` element is a unique identifier of the organization to which the project belongs. For our sample project, it is `org.packt.cookbook`. It is a good practice to follow the reverse domain name notation to specify this:

```
<groupId>...</groupId>
```

The `artifactId` element is the name of the project. For our sample project, it is `simple-project`:

```
<artifactId>...</artifactId>
```

The `version` element is the specific instance of the project, corresponding to the source code at a particular instance of time. In our case, it is `1.0-SNAPSHOT`, which is a default version during development:

```
<version>...</version>
```

We will explore the difference between the **SNAPSHOT** and concrete versions later in the book.

The combination of `groupId`, `artifactId`, and `version` uniquely identifies the project. In this sense, they are the coordinates of the project.

The `packaging` element indicates the artifact type of the project. This is typically a `jar`, `war`, `zip`, or in some cases, a `pom`:

```
<packaging>...</packaging>
```

The `dependencies` element section of the pom file defines all the dependent projects of this project. This would typically be third-party libraries required to build, test, and run the project:

```
<dependencies>...</dependencies>
```

The `parent` section is used to indicate a relationship, specifically a parent-child relationship. If the project is part of a multi-module project or inherits project information from another project, then the details are specified in this section:

```
<parent>...</parent>
```

Maven properties are **placeholders**. Their values are accessible anywhere in the pom file by using `${key}`, where `key` is the property name:

```
<properties>...</properties>
```

A project with modules is known as a multi-module or **aggregator project**. Modules are projects that this pom file lists and are executed as a group:

```
<modules>...</modules>
```

For more information on multi-module projects refer to *Chapter 9, Multi-module Projects*.

Understanding Maven settings

Now that we have got an idea of the essential elements of a pom file, let us also examine the various setting properties of Maven.

How to do it...

To understand the Maven settings, perform the following steps:

1. Open the `settings.xml` file in the `.m2` subfolder of your HOME folder, if it exists:

```
<settings xmlns="http://maven.apache.org/SETTINGS/1.0.0"
    xmlns:xsi="http://www.w3.org/2001/XMLSchema-instance"
    xsi:schemaLocation="http://maven.apache.org/SETTINGS/1.0.0
                        http://maven.apache.org/xsd/settings-1.0.0.xsd">
    <localRepository>C:/software/maven</localRepository>
    <pluginGroups>
        <pluginGroup>org.eclipse.jetty</pluginGroup>
        <pluginGroup>org.codehaus.cargo</pluginGroup>
        <pluginGroup>org.apache.tomcat.maven</pluginGroup>
        <pluginGroup>org.jacoco</pluginGroup>
    </pluginGroups>
</settings>
```

2. Otherwise, open the `settings.xml` file in the `conf` folder of your Maven installation (as defined in M2_HOME).

How it works...

Maven has a global settings file called `settings.xml` in the `conf` folder of the Maven installation. The values in this file can be overridden in the user settings file— the `settings.xml` file—that is present in the `.m2` subfolder of your HOME folder.

The settings file contains configurations that are not specific to a project, but are global in nature. It also contains information that is not meant to be distributed (for example, passwords).

Like the pom file, the settings file is also an XML file based on an XML schema. It starts as follows:

```
<settings xmlns="http://maven.apache.org/SETTINGS/1.0.0"
        xmlns:xsi="http://www.w3.org/2001/XMLSchema-instance"
        xsi:schemaLocation="http://maven.apache.org/SETTINGS/1.0.0
                        http://maven.apache.org/xsd/settings-
1.0.0.xsd">
```

Let us now see some of the typical setting configurations:

The localRepository element

The following code represents the `localRepository` element in the settings file:

```
<localRepository>${user.home}/.m2/repository</localRepository>
```

We have seen this in the *Changing the location of the Maven repository* recipe in *Chapter 1, Getting Started,* where we wanted to change the default location where Maven dependencies and plugins are stored.

The offline element

The following code represents the `offline` element in the settings file:

```
<offline>false</offline>
```

This setting indicates whether Maven should operate in offline mode; that is, it should not download updates or dependencies if they are not available.

The proxies element

We saw proxies in the **Running Maven behind an HTTP proxy server** recipe in *Chapter 1, Getting Started.* The following code represents the `proxies` element in the settings file:

```
<proxies>
    <proxy>
        <id>myproxy</id>
        <active>true</active>
        <protocol>http</protocol>
        <host>proxy.myorg.com</host>
        <port>8080</port>
        <username>proxyuser</username>
        <password>somepassword</password>
        <nonProxyHosts>*.myorg.com </nonProxyHosts>
    </proxy>
</proxies>
```

This allows us to specify a proxy server to connect to the Internet. This is relevant in enterprises where direct access to the Internet might be blocked due to security or other reasons.

The mirrors element

The following code represents the `mirrors` element in the settings file:

```
<mirror>
    <id>nexus</id>
    <name>My Company Mirror</name>
    <url>http://nexus.mycompany.com/pub/maven2</url>
    <mirrorOf>central</mirrorOf>
</mirror>
```

Instead of downloading dependencies from Maven Central, you can configure Maven to download them from a mirror of the central repository. This is extremely useful in an organization where the repository can be mirrored in a repository manager within an organization and all users can download dependencies from this mirror.

The repositories element

Repositories are remote collections of projects that Maven uses to populate the required dependencies to a local repository. There are two types of repositories—releases and snapshots—and Maven allows specific configurations for each, as illustrated in the following code:

```
<repositories>
      <repository>
        <id>codehausSnapshots</id>
        <name>Codehaus Snapshots</name>
        <releases>
          <enabled>false</enabled>
          <updatePolicy>always</updatePolicy>
          <checksumPolicy>warn</checksumPolicy>
        </releases>
        <snapshots>
          <enabled>true</enabled>
          <updatePolicy>never</updatePolicy>
          <checksumPolicy>fail</checksumPolicy>
        </snapshots>
        <url>http://snapshots.maven.codehaus.org/maven2</url>
        <layout>default</layout>
      </repository>
    </repositories>
```

The pluginRepositories element

While repositories store dependencies required for the project, the pluginRepositories element stores plugin libraries and associated files. Maven distinguishes between these two by having separate configurations for both. The elements are the same as that for repositories, except that the parent element is pluginRepositories.

The servers element

The repositories for download and deployment are defined by the `repositories` and `distributionManagement` elements of the pom file. However, settings such as `username` and `password` cannot be distributed in the pom file for confidentiality reasons. Maven provides a mechanism to specify this in the settings file:

```
<servers>
    <server>
        <id>server001</id>
        <username>my_login</username>
        <password>my_password</password>
        <privateKey>${user.home}/.ssh/id_dsa</privateKey>
        <passphrase>some_passphrase</passphrase>
        <filePermissions>664</filePermissions>
        <directoryPermissions>775</directoryPermissions>
        <configuration></configuration>
    </server>
</servers>
```

Understanding command-line options in Maven

While the most popular way to run Maven is to specify goals, Maven provides a number of command-line options to customize its behavior. They range from specifying values for properties, to varying the verbosity of the Maven output. It is useful to know some of the arguments, as they will often help with troubleshooting issues with Maven.

Getting ready

Maven is set up on your system and is verified as working.

How to do it...

To understand command-line options in Maven, perform the following steps:

1. Open the command prompt.
2. Run the following command:

   ```
   mvn -h
   ```

3. You will see an output such as the following screenshot:

```
C:\projects\apache-maven-cookbook>mvn -h

usage: mvn [options] [<goal(s)>] [<phase(s)>]

Options:
 -am,--also-make                        If project list is specified, also
                                        build projects required by the
                                        list
 -amd,--also-make-dependents            If project list is specified, also
                                        build projects that depend on
                                        projects on the list
 -B,--batch-mode                        Run in non-interactive (batch)
                                        mode
 -b,--builder <arg>                     The id of the build strategy to
                                        use.
 -C,--strict-checksums                  Fail the build if checksums don't
                                        match
 -c,--lax-checksums                     Warn if checksums don't match
 -cpu,--check-plugin-updates            Ineffective, only kept for
                                        backward compatibility
 -D,--define <arg>                      Define a system property
 -e,--errors                            Produce execution error messages
 -emp,--encrypt-master-password <arg>   Encrypt master security password
 -ep,--encrypt-password <arg>           Encrypt server password
 -f,--file <arg>                        Force the use of an alternate POM
                                        file (or directory with pom.xml).
 -fae,--fail-at-end                     Only fail the build afterwards;
                                        allow all non-impacted builds to
                                        continue
 -ff,--fail-fast                        Stop at first failure in
                                        reactorized builds
```

A number of options that Maven supports are displayed in the preceding screenshot.

How it works...

We will briefly discuss the command-line options that Maven provides.

Options

When there is an error while running Maven, this flag will result in Maven displaying a detailed stack trace of the error:

`-e -errors`

When the `quiet` option is enabled, only errors are displayed. The other outputs are not printed. This permits speeding up builds where verbose outputs are usually displayed:

`-q -quiet`

We have seen the `version` option to display the Maven version in the first three recipes of *Chapter 1, Getting Started*. This is also a simple way to check if Maven is installed and working:

`-v -version`

When invoked with the `offline` option, Maven does not attempt to download any dependency or plugin from the Internet. This option will work correctly, provided Maven has all the information required for the project to be built and run. We will see how to enable projects to run in offline mode:

```
-o –offline
```

When enabled with the `debug` option, Maven prints a lot of verbose output about every step that it performs. This is typically used to troubleshoot any build issues:

```
-X –debug
```

Understanding Maven profiles

Maven is designed to create portable builds that are expected to work across different platforms and in various runtime environments.

Now, there may be situations where you need to build the same project differently. For instance, you may need to build a project differently for the purpose of staging and production. You may not want to build a project that requires a Linux library on Windows.

How to do it...

Let's understand Maven profiles by performing the following steps:

1. Open `settings.xml` in the `conf` subfolder of your Maven installation (as specified in `M2_HOME`).
2. View the commented section of profiles.

How it works...

Maven provides three type of profiles:

- ▶ Per Project profile as defined in the pom file of the project
- ▶ Per User profile as defined in the user settings file (in the `.m2` subfolder of the user's `HOME` folder)
- ▶ A Global profile as defined in the global settings file (in the `conf` folder of `M2_HOME`)

By creating different profiles for different variations of the project build, you can use the same pom file to create differing builds.

One should be careful to ensure that this does not result in a non-portable build.

Adding a new Maven profile

Let us add a simple Maven profile to test our understanding of profiles.

How to do it...

Let's create a new Maven profile, by performing the following steps:

1. Create a new Maven project using the commands specified in the *Creating a simple project with Maven* recipe in *Chapter 1, Getting Started.*

2. Add the following code in the `pom.xml` file:

```
<profiles>
      <profile>
          <id>dev</id>
          <activation>
              <activeByDefault>false</activeByDefault>
          </activation>
      </profile>
</profiles>
```

How it works...

There are two ways to create a profile: in the project's pom file or in the settings file. It is important to note that, if a profile is active from the settings file, its values will override any profiles with equivalent IDs in the pom file.

The profile in `pom.xml` can have the following elements:

```
<profile>
      <id>test</id>
      <activation>...</activation>
      <build>...</build>
      <modules>...</modules>
      <repositories>...</repositories>
      <pluginRepositories>...</pluginRepositories>
      <dependencies>...</dependencies>
      <reporting>...</reporting>
      <dependencyManagement>...</dependencyManagement>
      <distributionManagement>...</distributionManagement>
</profile>
```

The profile in `settings.xml` can only have the following elements:

```
<profile>
    <id>test</id>
    <activation>...</activation>
    <repositories>...</repositories>
    <pluginRepositories>...</pluginRepositories>
    <properties>...</properties>
    </profile>
```

See also

▶   The *Activating/deactivating a Maven profile* recipe in this chapter

Activating/deactivating a Maven profile

A profile can be specified in `pom.xml` or `settings.xml`. Each profile may be created for a specific purpose; for instance, to run on a particular platform or to run in an integration environment. All profiles may not need to run in all cases. Maven provides a mechanism to activate and deactivate a profile as required.

Getting ready

Use the project where we created the profile to add a new Maven profile section.

How to do it...

Let's perform the following steps to activate/deactivate a Maven profile:

1. To deactivate a profile, set the following value in the `activeByDefault` element:

    `<activeByDefault>false</activeByDefault>`

2. Run the Maven command to check if the profile is active:

    mvn help:active-profiles

    The output for the preceding command is shown as follows:

    [INFO] --- maven-help-plugin:2.2:active-profiles (default-cli) @ project-with-profile ---

    [INFO]

```
Active Profiles for Project 'com.packt.cookbook:project-with-
profile:jar:1.0-SNAPSHOT':
The following profiles are active:
```

3. To activate the profile, set the following value:

   ```
   <activeByDefault>true</activeByDefault>
   ```

4. Confirm that the profile is now active, by executing the following command:

   ```
   mvn help:active-profiles
   ```

   The output for preceding command is shown as follows:

   ```
   The following profiles are active:

   - dev (source: com.packt.cookbook:project-with-profile:1.0-
   SNAPSHOT)
   ```

How it works...

Profiles can be triggered in one of the following ways:

- Explicitly: Here, Maven provides a command-line option to invoke a profile, shown in the following command:

  ```
  mvn -P dev package
  ```

  This invokes the dev profile

- Through settings: A profile can be activated in the settings file by setting the <active> property to true. If activated, when the project is built, the profile is invoked:

  ```
  <activeProfiles>
    <activeProfile>dev</activeProfile>
  </activeProfiles>
  ```

- Based on environment variables: The profile can be activated based on any environment variable and the value that it has:

  ```
  <profile>
      <activation>
        <property>
          <name>debug</name>
        </property>
      </activation>
      ...
  </profile>
  ```

If the system property `debug` is defined and has any value, then the profile is activated

▶ Based on OS settings: The following profile will only run on Windows:

```
<profile>
    <activation>
      <os>
        <family>Windows</family>
      </os>
    </activation>
    ...
  </profile>
```

▶ Present or missing files: The following profile will be activated if the `target/site` file is missing:

```
<profile>
    <activation>
      <file>
        <missing>target/site</missing>
      </file>
    </activation>
  </profile>
```

Using properties in Maven

Maven allows us to define as well as use properties. Properties allow us to avoid hardcoding values in multiple places such as versions of dependencies. They also provide flexibility to the build tool by allowing values to be passed at runtime.

How to do it...

Let's define and use Maven properties by performing the following steps:

1. Open the pom file of a project that we created earlier.

2. Define a property:

```
<properties>
    <junit.version>3.8.1</junit.version>
  </properties>
```

3. Use the property:

```
<dependency>
        <groupId>junit</groupId>
        <artifactId>junit</artifactId>
        <version>${junit.version}</version>
        <scope>test</scope>
    </dependency>
```

How it works...

There are different types of properties. They are as follows:

*   Environment variables: Prefixing a variable with `env.` will return the value of the shell's environment variable. For example, `${env.PATH}` will return the value of the `PATH` variable.

*   pom variables: Prefixing a variable with `project.` will return the value of that element in the pom file. For example, `${project.version}` will return the value in the `<version>` tag of the pom file.

*   The `settings` variable: Prefixing a variable with `settings.` will return the value of that element in the settings file. For example, `${settings.offline}` will return the value `<offline>` in the settings file.

*   Java properties: Any property available through the `System.getProperties()` method in Java is available. For example, `${java.home}`.

*   Normal properties: Values that are specified in the `<properties>` tag, which is shown in the following example:

```
<properties>
    <java.version>1.7</java.version>
</properties>
```

Here, the `${java.version}` command will return `1.7`

Do remember that properties and profiles can break the portability of the project. Two specific practices for looking up in problem areas are as follows:

*   External properties: These are properties defined outside the pom file (in a settings file) but used as part of a plugin configuration. The absence of this property definition will break the build.

*   Incomplete specification: This is where properties are defined for different build environments. A missing definition for one will break the build.

See also

▶ The *Specifying source encoding for platform-independent builds* recipe in this chapter.

Specifying source encoding for platform-independent builds

Let us put our learning of properties to practical use. You will have observed the following warning while building the simple project that we created in the *Building a simple project with Maven* recipe in *Chapter 1, Getting Started*:

```
[WARNING] Using platform encoding (Cp1252 actually) to copy filtered
resources,
```

```
i.e. build is platform dependent!
```

Let us remove this warning if we really do not want the build to be platform dependent.

How to do it...

Let's specify the source encoding for platform-independent builds in our Maven project, by performing the following steps:

1. Open the pom file we created previously.

2. Add the following code:

```
<properties>
       <project.build.sourceEncoding>UTF-8
</project.build.sourceEncoding>
   </properties>
```

3. Run the following command:

   mvn package

4. Observe that the warning is no longer present.

How it works...

The `project.build.sourceEncoding` property explicitly specifies the encoding of the source files. Maven plugins get information about the encoding from the value of this property and use it.

This value will be the same on any platform that the project is built on and, thus, the build becomes independent of the platform.

4

Essential Maven Plugins

In this chapter, we will look at the following recipes:

- ▸ Using the Maven Clean plugin
- ▸ Using the Maven Compiler plugin
- ▸ Changing the compiler used by the Maven Compiler plugin
- ▸ Specifying the Java version for the Compiler plugin
- ▸ Using the Maven Surefire plugin to run unit tests
- ▸ Using the Maven Failsafe plugin to run integration tests
- ▸ Using the Maven Resources plugin
- ▸ Filtering using resources
- ▸ Using Eclipse to run Maven goals
- ▸ Using NetBeans to run Maven goals
- ▸ Using IntelliJ IDEA to run Maven goals

Introduction

In the previous chapter, we learned about the Maven lifecycle and the phases and goals of the lifecycle, understood the essential elements of the pom project configuration file and the settings file, and learned to use Maven profiles and properties.

In this chapter, we will look at how to add and configure plugins to the pom file and use them to perform essential build tasks. Maven has a plugin architecture, and except for core functionalities, every task in Maven is done using plugins. There are a number of plugins that are provided by Maven. In addition, there are several third-party plugins. Maven also provides a mechanism for users to develop their own plugins if they choose to do so.

Using the Maven Clean plugin

When a project is built, it is important to ensure that it is not adversely affected by artifacts of an earlier build. Usually, build tools generate artifacts in a well-defined folder, namely the `target` folder, called **project working directory**. Before a new build, this folder is usually deleted.

Getting ready

Maven is set up on your system and is verified to work. To do this, refer to the first three recipes of *Chapter 1, Getting Started*.

How to do it...

Let's start using the Maven Clean plugin by performing the following steps:

1. Open the command prompt.

2. Run the following Maven command in the simple Maven project that we created in the *Creating a simple project with Maven* recipe in *Chapter 1, Getting Started*:

   ```
   mvn clean
   ```

3. Observe the various steps that get executed:

   ```
   [INFO] --- maven-clean-plugin:2.4.1:clean (default-clean) @
   simple-project ---
   [INFO] Deleting C:\projects\apache-maven-cookbook\simple-
   project\target
   ```

   If there are no files/folders to delete, you will not see the following output:

   ```
   [INFO] --- maven-clean-plugin:2.5:clean (default-clean) @
   simple-project ---
   [INFO] -----------------------------------------------------------
   ----------------
   [INFO] BUILD SUCCESS
   ```

How it works...

When the `clean` phase is invoked, Maven automatically infers that the `clean` lifecycle is invoked.

It uses the Maven Clean plugin for this. The plugin has only one goal, namely `clean`, to clean the working directory.

In the case of Maven, the working directory is called `target`. Maven creates this directory when a build is done. The `clean` goal of the plugin attempts to delete this directory.

As `clean` is a separate lifecycle from the `default` (build) lifecycle, `clean` needs to be explicitly called before the `default` lifecycle if you need to ensure that the working directory is removed.

There's more...

In this section, we will discuss how to run the Clean plugin automatically during the build, the steps to skip the deletion of working directory, and the process of deleting some additional files/folders.

Cleaning automatically

In the previous example, as we used the default behavior of the plugin and did not need to make any configurations, we did not need to make any change to the pom configuration file. However, what if we want to ensure that the `clean` goal is run without explicitly calling it?

To do this, we need to define the plugin with some parameters in our pom file:

1. Let us add the following code in our pom file:

    ```
    <build>
        <plugins>
            <plugin>
                <artifactId>maven-clean-plugin</artifactId>
                <version>2.6</version>
                <executions>
                    <execution>
                        <id>auto-clean</id>
                        <phase>initialize</phase>
                        <goals>
                            <goal>clean</goal>
                        </goals>
                    </execution>
                </executions>
            </plugin>
        </plugins>
    </build>
    ```

    Though the preceding declaration may look verbose, all we are asking is for the `clean` goal to be invoked during the `initialize` phase of the project. We are identifying this `execution` with an `id` called `auto-clean`.

2. Now run the following command on the command prompt:

   `mvn package`

3. You will see the following screenshot:

```
C:\projects\apache-maven-cookbook\project-with-autoclean>mvn package
[INFO] Scanning for projects...
[INFO]
[INFO]
[INFO] ----------------------------------------------------------------
[INFO] Building Project with autoclean 1.0-SNAPSHOT
[INFO] ----------------------------------------------------------------
[INFO]
[INFO]
[INFO] --- maven-clean-plugin:2.6:clean (auto-clean) @ project-with-autoclean --

[INFO] Deleting C:\projects\apache-maven-cookbook\project-with-autoclean\target
[INFO]
[INFO] --- maven-resources-plugin:2.6:resources (default-resources) @ project-wi
th-autoclean ---
```

Even though we did not call the `clean` phase, the `clean` goal got invoked because it was configured in the pom file to run in the `initialize` phase.

Skipping the deletion of the working directory

Let us look at the converse of the preceding use case. For some reason, we do not want the working directory to be deleted, even if `clean` is run. To do this, perform the following steps:

1. Configure the plugin as follows:

   ```
   <plugin>
     <artifactId>maven-clean-plugin</artifactId>
     <version>2.6</version>
     <configuration>
       <skip>true</skip>
     </configuration>
   </plugin>
   ```

2. Run the following command on the command prompt:

   `mvn clean`

3. Observe the output, which is as follows:

   ```
   C:\projects\apache-maven-cookbook\project-with-clean-
   disabled>mvn clean

   [INFO] Scanning for projects...

   [INFO]

   [INFO] -------------------------------------------------------------
   -------------

   [INFO] Building Project with clean disabled 1.0-SNAPSHOT
   ```

```
[INFO] ------------------------------------------------------------
-----------------
[INFO]
[INFO] --- maven-clean-plugin:2.6:clean (default-clean) @
project-with-clean-disabled ---
[INFO] Clean is skipped.
```

Setting the `skip` plugin property to `true` indicates to Maven that the `clean` goal must be skipped.

Deleting additional folders/files

What if your project has an additional folder, say `report`, besides `target`, which is perhaps created by another script, and you want that to be deleted as well? We use the following steps to do the same:

1. Configure the plugin as follows:

   ```xml
   <plugin>
     <artifactId>maven-clean-plugin</artifactId>
     <version>2.6</version>
     <configuration>
       <filesets>
         <fileset>
           <directory>${basedir}/report</directory>
         </fileset>
       </filesets>
     </configuration>
   </plugin>
   ```

   You have now configured the plugin to delete an additional directory

2. Create a `report` folder for the purpose of testing.

3. Run the following command on command prompt:

   `mvn clean`

4. You will now see the following output:

   ```
   C:\projects\apache-maven-cookbook\project-with-clean-
   additional-folder>mvn clean

   [INFO] Scanning for projects...

   [INFO]

   [INFO] ------------------------------------------------------------
   -----------------

   [INFO] Building Project with clean additional folder 1.0-
   SNAPSHOT
   ```

```
[INFO] ---------------------------------------------------------
-----------------
[INFO]
[INFO] --- maven-clean-plugin:2.6:clean (default-clean) @
project-with-clean-additional-folder ---
[INFO] Deleting C:\projects\apache-maven-cookbook\project-
with-clean-additional-folder\report (includes = [], excludes =
[])
```

The `report` folder is deleted as well. In fact, Maven can be configured to delete (or not delete) specific folders and files inside that folder as well.

Using the Maven Compiler plugin

Compilation is an essential task performed by a build tool. Maven uses the Maven Compiler plugin to do the compilation. The plugin provides several configurations to make the compilation flexible.

How to do it...

To use the Maven Compiler plugin, perform the following steps:

1. Open a command prompt.

2. Run the following Maven command on the simple project that we created in the *Creating a simple project with Maven* recipe in *Chapter 1, Getting Started*:

   `mvn compile`

3. Observe the output, which is as follows:

   ```
   [INFO] --- maven-compiler-plugin:2.3.2:compile (default-
   compile) @ simple-project ---
   [INFO] Compiling 1 source file to C:\projects\apache-maven-
   cookbook\simple-project\target\classes
   ```

How it works...

The `compile` parameter indicates the invocation of the `default` lifecycle to Maven. As illustrated in the *Understanding the Maven lifecycle, phases, and goals* recipe in *Chapter 3, Maven Lifecycle*, Maven runs all the phases up to and including the `compile` phase in order.

The `compile` phase itself essentially runs the `compile` goal of the Maven Compiler plugin.

This compiles the Java source files to classes in the `target/classes` folder.

One question would have struck you. What about the test classes? Why does the `compile` phase not compile the test sources?

The answer lies in the way Maven handles the lifecycle and phases of the lifecycle. Why would you want to compile the test sources unless you want to run the tests?

There's more...

What if we want to compile the test sources?

Let us try running the following command on the command prompt:

`mvn test`

Observe the output as shown in the following screenshot:

```
[INFO]
[INFO] --- maven-compiler-plugin:3.1:testCompile (default-testCompile) @ simple-
project ---
[INFO] Changes detected - recompiling the module!
[WARNING] File encoding has not been set, using platform encoding Cp1252, i.e. b
uild is platform dependent!
[INFO] Compiling 1 source file to C:\projects\apache-maven-cookbook\simple-proje
ct\target\test-classes
[INFO]
[INFO] --- maven-surefire-plugin:2.12.4:test (default-test) @ simple-project ---
```

As we specified the `test` phase, Maven ran all phases prior to it, which includes compiling the test sources using the `testCompile` goal of the Maven Compiler plugin.

Changing the compiler used by the Maven Compiler plugin

Let us say we are running Maven using JDK 7 but our project requires the sources to be compiled using JDK 8. Essentially, we want to use a JDK for compilation that is different from the JDK running Maven.

In this case, we can specify the compiler we want to use to Maven.

How to do it...

Use the following steps to change the compiler used by the Maven Compiler plugin:

1. Open the command prompt.

2. Define a Maven property to store the location details for Java 8:

```
<properties>
    <JAVA8.HOME>C:/Program
Files/Java/jdk1.8.0_20</JAVA8.HOME>
</properties>
```

> The portable way to do this would be to define this property in a `profile` in the user's `settings.xml` file. This is because the location of `JAVA_HOME` may be different for different users based on their operating system or preferred installation location.

3. Add the following plugin configuration to the Maven project:

```
<plugins>
  <plugin>
    <groupId>org.apache.maven.plugins</groupId>
    <artifactId>maven-compiler-plugin</artifactId>
    <version>3.2</version>
    <configuration>
      <verbose>true</verbose>
      <fork>true</fork>
      <executable>${JAVA8.HOME}/bin/javac</executable>
      <compilerVersion>1.8</compilerVersion>
    </configuration>
  </plugin>
</plugins>
```

> The `fork` element needs to be set to `true` for the preceding code to work. Maven will invoke the different java compiler in a separate thread and hence the need to fork. This is so that Maven can load a different JVM corresponding to a different JDK.

4. Run the following command on a command prompt:

```
mvn compile
```

How it works...

There would no visible difference in the way the compilation happens, except that now, the compiler specified in the `executable` element will get invoked.

See also

▸ The *Specifying the Java version for the Compiler plugin* recipe in this chapter

Specifying the Java version for the Compiler plugin

When we created a new project in Eclipse, you would have observed the following warning:

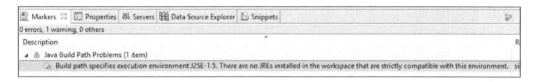

Why does this error occur? This is because the Maven Compiler plugin, by default, considers the `source` and `target` Java version to be `1.5` (for backward compatibility reasons).

Let us resolve this warning.

How to do it...

Let us assume you have configured Java 8 as the default Java runtime in Eclipse, and perform the following steps:

1. Open the Eclipse project.

2. Add the following configuration to the Maven Compiler plugin:

```
<plugins>
  <plugin>
    <groupId>org.apache.maven.plugins</groupId>
    <artifactId>maven-compiler-plugin</artifactId>
    <version>3.2</version>
    <configuration>
      <source>1.8</source>
      <target>1.8</target>
    </configuration>
  </plugin>
</plugins>
```

3. Alternately, add the following properties in the `properties` element (this is essentially a shortcut for the earlier process):

```
<properties>
    <maven.compiler.target>1.8</maven.compiler.target>
    <maven.compiler.source>1.8</maven.compiler.source>
</properties>
```

4. Check if the warning goes away.

How it works...

When the `source` and `target` versions of Java are explicitly set to the compiler, the version of java used in the source code as well as the desired version of the compiled classes are unambiguous. There is no likelihood of the compiler compiling to the incorrect target version of Java.

Consequently, the Eclipse warning goes away.

There's more...

You may need to pass compiler arguments in the `compilerArguement` element to the compiler. For instance, you may want to identify the usage of deprecated APIs in the code. You can do this by adding the following configuration:

```
<plugin>
    <groupId>org.apache.maven.plugins</groupId>
    <artifactId>maven-compiler-plugin</artifactId>
    <version>3.2</version>
    <configuration>
        <compilerArgument>-Xlint:deprecation</compilerArgument>
    </configuration>
</plugin>
```

When run on a code that has a deprecation, you can see the relevant lines:

```
[INFO] Compiling 1 source file to C:\projects\apache-maven-
cookbook\project-with-deprecation\target\classes

[WARNING] /C:/projects/apache-maven-cookbook/project-with-
deprecation/src/main/java/com/packt/cookbook/App.java:[12,24]
Date(int,int,int) in java.util.Date has been deprecated
```

Using the Maven Surefire plugin to run unit tests

A best practice of software development is writing automated unit tests for the code that you develop. Let us now see how to run these tests.

The plugin that does this job is the Maven Surefire plugin.

How to do it...

To run unit tests using the Maven Surefire plugin, perform the following steps:

1. Open the command prompt.

2. Run the following command on one of our sample projects:

   `mvn test`

3. Observe the various steps that get executed:

   ```
   [INFO] --- maven-surefire-plugin:2.10:test (default-test) @
   simple-project ---

   [INFO] Surefire report directory: C:\projects\apache-maven-
   cookbook\simple-project\target\surefire-reports

   -------------------------------------------------------------

    T E S T S

   -------------------------------------------------------------

   Running com.packt.cookbook.AppTest

   Tests run: 1, Failures: 0, Errors: 0, Skipped: 0, Time
   elapsed: 0 sec

   Results:

   Tests run: 1, Failures: 0, Errors: 0, Skipped: 0
   ```

How it works...

The `test` parameter indicates the invocation of the `default` lifecycle to Maven. As illustrated in the *Understanding the Maven lifecycle, phases, and goals* recipe in *Chapter 3, Maven Lifecycle*, Maven runs all the phases up to and including the `test` phase, in order.

The `test` phase itself essentially runs the `test` goal of the Maven Surefire plugin.

This runs the test classes that are present in the `target/test-classes` folder.

The test that we have is a test written using the JUnit framework. Not only does the plugin run the test, it also generates a test report that can be used to analyze failures as well as test coverage.

Check the `surefire-reports` folder:

```
C:\projects\apache-maven-cookbook\simple-project\target\surefire-reports>dir
 Volume in drive C has no label.
 Volume Serial Number is 04B8-E184

 Directory of C:\projects\apache-maven-cookbook\simple-project\target\surefire-r
eports

16-02-2015  08:08 PM    <DIR>          .
16-02-2015  08:08 PM    <DIR>          ..
16-02-2015  08:08 PM               274 com.packt.cookbook.AppTest.txt
16-02-2015  08:08 PM             6,274 TEST-com.packt.cookbook.AppTest.xml
               2 File(s)          6,548 bytes
```

While the text file contains the summary report, the XML file has the details of each of the tests.

There's more...

The Surefire plugin provides many configurations to make testing easier.

Using TestNG

JUnit is not the only way to write automated unit tests. You could use TestNG (`http://testng.org`) or even write your tests without using any framework (by using Java asserts).

Surefire determines the framework to be used based on the dependencies that have been defined.

Our earlier example ran JUnit tests because we had defined the `junit` dependency in the pom file.

Let us now write a test using TestNG and see what needs to change for it to work. Refer to the Maven project with TestNG.

The only change in the pom file is to replace the `junit` dependency with `testng`:

```
<dependency>
    <groupId>org.testng</groupId>
    <artifactId>testng</artifactId>
    <version>6.8.8</version>
    <scope>test</scope>
</dependency>
```

Run the following command on command prompt:

`mvn test`

The tests are now run in using TestNG:

```
[INFO]
[INFO] --- maven-surefire-plugin:2.10:test (default-test) @ project-
with-testNG---
[INFO] Surefire report directory: C:\projects\apache-maven-
cookbook\project-with-testNG\target\surefire-reports
-------------------------------------------------------
T E S T S
-------------------------------------------------------
Running com.packt.cookbook.AppTest
Set up run
Fast test
Slow test
Tests run: 2, Failures: 0, Errors: 0, Skipped: 0, Time elapsed: 0.609
sec
```

Now, examine the `surefire-reports` folder. It has a different set of files corresponding to `testng`:

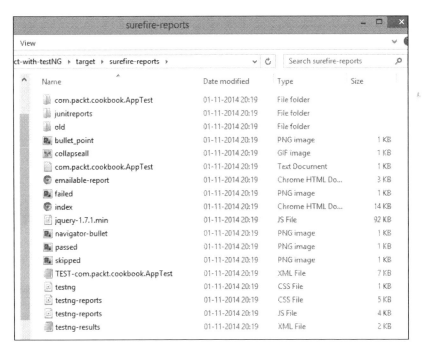

The same tests work with TestNG and JUnit as TestNG can run JUnit tests.

Skipping tests

There may be situations where you might not want to run the tests; some tests are possibly broken. This can be done in the following ways:

  ▸ Configuring the Surefire plugin in the pom file: Configure your Surefire plugin in the pom.xml file using the following code:

```
<plugins>
  <plugin>
    <groupId>org.apache.maven.plugins</groupId>
    <artifactId>maven-surefire-plugin</artifactId>
    <version>2.17</version>
    <configuration>
      <skipTests>true</skipTests>
    </configuration>
  </plugin>
</plugins>
```

  Now, run the following command:

  `mvn test`

  You will see the following output:

```
[INFO]
[INFO] --- maven-surefire-plugin:2.17:test (default-test) @
project-with-tests-skipped ---
[INFO] Tests are skipped.
```

  ▸ Issuing an `mvn` command with a command-line parameter: The tests can be skipped even by issuing the following command:

  `mvn -DskipTests tests`

Skipping the compilation of test sources

The skipTests parameter used in the preceding mvn command skips running of tests, but the test sources still get compiled by the earlier phases/goals. To skip the compilation of test sources, you can run the following command:

`mvn -Dmaven.test.skip=true package`

This will completely skip the test compilation and test execution.

Using the Maven Failsafe plugin to run integration tests

In addition to unit tests, Maven also allows you to automate the running of your integration tests. While unit tests are run during the `test` phase of the build lifecycle, integration tests are run during the `verify` phase. The Maven Failsafe plugin is used to run integration tests.

How to do it...

To run integration tests using Maven Failsafe plugin, perform the following steps:

1. Open a project containing integration tests, namely `project-with-integration-test`.

2. Add the following plugin configuration to the pom file:

```
<plugin>
    <groupId>org.apache.maven.plugins</groupId>
    <artifactId>maven-failsafe-plugin</artifactId>
    <version>2.18</version>
    <executions>
        <execution>
            <id>integration-tests</id>
            <goals>
                <goal>integration-test</goal>
                <goal>verify</goal>
            </goals>
        </execution>
    </executions>
</plugin>
```

3. Run the following command:

   mvn verify

4. Observe the various steps that get executed:

```
[INFO]
[INFO] --- maven-failsafe-plugin:2.18:integration-test (integration-tests) @ pro
ject-with-integration-tests ---
[INFO] Failsafe report directory: C:\projects\apache-maven-cookbook\project-with
-integration-tests\target\failsafe-reports

-------------------------------------------------------
 T E S T S
-------------------------------------------------------
Running com.packt.cookbook.AppIT
Tests run: 1, Failures: 0, Errors: 0, Skipped: 0, Time elapsed: 0 sec - in com.p
ackt.cookbook.AppIT

Results :

Tests run: 1, Failures: 0, Errors: 0, Skipped: 0

[WARNING] File encoding has not been set, using platform encoding Cp1252, i.e. b
uild is platform dependent!
[INFO]
[INFO] --- maven-failsafe-plugin:2.18:verify (integration-tests) @ project-with-
integration-tests ---
[INFO] Failsafe report directory: C:\projects\apache-maven-cookbook\project-with
-integration-tests\target\failsafe-reports
[WARNING] File encoding has not been set, using platform encoding Cp1252, i.e. b
uild is platform dependent!
```

How it works...

We have specified in the pom file that the integration test must be run and the goals of the Maven Failsafe plugin must be verified. These goals are bound to the `verify` phase of Maven and get invoked.

Using the Maven Resources plugin

The Resources plugin comes into picture to copy project resources to the output directory. The resources can be for the project to run or for the purpose of testing.

How to do it...

Let's start using the Maven Resources plugin by performing the following steps:

1. Open the command prompt.
2. Run the following command on the simple project that we created earlier:

   ```
   mvn process-resources
   ```

3. Observe what happens:

    ```
    [INFO] --- maven-resources-plugin:2.5:resources (default-
    resources) @ simple-project ---
    ```

    ```
    [INFO] skip non existing resourceDirectory C:\projects\apache-
    maven-cookbook\simple-project\src\main\resources
    ```

How it works...

When we specify the `process-resources` phase, Maven executes the `resources` goal of `maven-resources-plugin`, which is bound to the `process-resources` lifecycle phase.

In the earlier project, there are no resources and hence, resources are not copied.

If you add a file in `src\main\resources` (as in the case of the `project-with-resources` project), you will see the following output:

```
[INFO] --- maven-resources-plugin:2.5:resources (default-resources) @
project-with-properties ---
```

```
[INFO] Copying 1 resource
```

You could also explicitly invoke the plugin's goal as follows:

```
mvn resources:resources
```

You could also invoke any phase following the `process-resources` phase, which will trigger resource processing as well:

```
mvn compile
```

There is a separate goal to copy test resources to provide separation of the main and test resources. Like project resources, the test resource processing can be invoked in three ways, which are as follows:

- By specifying a phase that will automatically invoke phases before it:

  ```
  mvn process-test-resources
  ```

- By explicitly stating the plugin's goal:

  ```
  mvn resources:testResources
  ```

- By a phase following `process-test-resources`:

  ```
  mvn test
  ```

There's more...

What if we had resources in additional folders? The Maven Resources plugin allows us to configure these additional folders.

Let's say we have an additional resources folder, namely `src/main/additional`. We can configure the `pom.xml` file as follows:

```
<build>
    <resources>
      <resource>
          <directory>src/main/resources</directory>
      </resource>
      <resource>
          <directory>src/main/additional</directory>
      </resource>
    </resources>
    </build>
```

Now, run the following command:

`mvn process-resources`

Observe the output:

```
[INFO] --- maven-resources-plugin:2.5:resources (default-resources) @
project-with-additional-resources ---

[INFO] Copying 1 resource

[INFO] Copying 1 resource
```

The line `Copying 1 resource` repeats twice, indicating the copying happening from two folders.

Filtering using resources

Now, let us see how we can put the resources features of Maven to good use, that is, to perform variable replacements on project resources. This feature is useful when you need to parameterize a build with different configuration values, depending on the deployment platform.

You can define variables in your resources. Let us see how we can get the value of these variables from properties, resource filter files, and the command line.

How to do it...

To perform filtering using resources, use the following steps:

1. Add a property with a variable in the `src/main/resource/app.properties` file:

   ```
   display.name=Hello ${project.name}
   ```

2. Add the following code in the pom file:

   ```
   <build>
     <resources>
       <resource>
         <directory>src/main/resources</directory>
         <filtering>true</filtering>
       </resource>
     </resources>
   </build>
   ```

3. Invoke the `process-resources` phase:

   ```
   mvn process-resources
   ```

4. Examine the processed resource `app.properties` in `target/classes`:

   ```
   C:\projects\apache-maven-cookbook\project-with-resource-
   filtering\target\classes>type app.properties

   display.name=Hello Project with resource filtering
   ```

How it works...

In the *Using properties in Maven* recipe of *Chapter 3, Maven Lifecycle*, we saw the various types of properties that Maven can have. In the preceding case, we set the `filtering` element to `true`. Maven replaced the variable `${project.name}` with the property value corresponding to the name of the project defined in the pom file, namely `Project with resource filtering`.

There's more...

You can override the property values from the command line:

```
mvn -Dproject.name="Override from command line" process-resources
```

Now, look at `app.properties` by navigating to `target/classes`:

```
C:\projects\apache-maven-cookbook\project-with-resource-
filtering>type target\classes\app.properties

display.name=Hello Override from command line
```

If you have a large number of variables whose values differ based on the environment, then you can create a file, say `my-filter-values.properties`, in the project codebase holding the keys and values (say, `src/filter` folder) and use them as filters:

```
<filters>
    <filter>my-filter-values.properties</filter>
</filters>
```

Using Eclipse to run Maven goals

If you are using Eclipse to develop your project, it is good to know how to run some of the plugins we have discussed earlier using the IDE.

How to do it...

To run Maven goals using Eclipse, use the following steps:

1. Open the simple project in Eclipse.

2. Right-click on the project.

3. Choose **Run As**.

4. View the available Maven options:

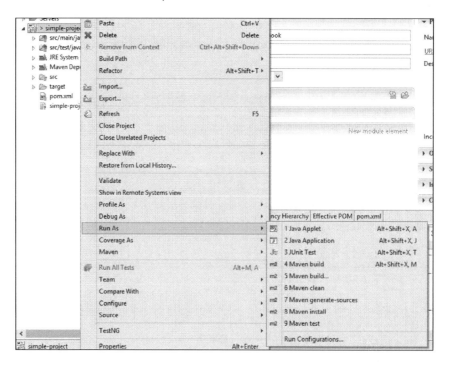

How it works...

Eclipse provides an option to run various goals from the IDE. Among the ones we have seen in this chapter, `clean`, `compile`, and `test` are offered by Eclipse. There are a few other options as well.

In addition, Eclipse also allows us to modify the configurations as suitable.

Eclipse also allows the project to be **Run As** a **Java Application** in the traditional way (without using any Maven plugins). Likewise, it allows a **JUnit Test** to be run without using Maven.

Using NetBeans to run Maven goals

Let us now see how we can run the Maven goals in NetBeans.

How to do it...

To run Maven goals using the NetBeans IDE, implement the following steps:

1. Open the simple project in the NetBeans IDE.
2. Right-click on the project.
3. View the available options:

How it works...

Unlike Eclipse, NetBeans has a tighter Maven integration. This means each of the menu options (**Build**, **Clean and Build**, **Clean**, and so on) call the corresponding Maven command to do so.

For instance, clicking on the **Clean** option will result in the following:

As can be seen, it runs the `mvn clean` command.

Similarly, the **Clean and Build** option is equivalent to the `mvn clean install` command.

These are simple use cases. NetBeans provides additional configuration options to override default Maven behavior.

Using IntelliJ IDEA to run Maven goals

Finally, let us look at what IntelliJ IDEA provides.

How to do it...

To run Maven goals using IntelliJ IDEA, perform the following steps:

1. Open the simple project in IntelliJ IDEA.

2. Select **Maven Projects**:

3. Open **Lifecycle** and click on a suitable goal/phase:

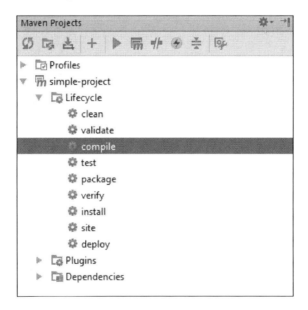

How it works...

Clicking on a Maven phase/goal invokes the corresponding Maven command and the same is executed. For instance, clicking on **compile** does the following:

There are also other configuration options provided by IntelliJ IDEA to customize Maven projects.

5

Dependency Management

In this chapter, we will cover the following recipes:

- ▶ Choosing the scope of dependency
- ▶ Getting a report of dependencies
- ▶ Getting into dependency and avoiding dependency hell
- ▶ Downloading dependencies into a folder
- ▶ Understanding SNAPSHOT dependencies
- ▶ Handling dependency download errors
- ▶ Detecting unused/undeclared dependencies
- ▶ Manually installing dependencies that are not available in a repository
- ▶ Dependency management using Eclipse
- ▶ Dependency management using NetBeans
- ▶ Dependency management using IntelliJ IDEA

Introduction

One of the powerful features of Maven is managing the dependencies required by the project. It is rare for a project to be developed without using other dependencies. The typical issues in using dependencies relate to the number and choice of dependencies, their versions, and the transitive dependencies (a project dependency, in turn, being dependent on other dependencies).

Maven has a way of managing the dependencies, as well as providing users with enough flexibility to handle complexities, as they arise.

Choosing the scope of dependency

We may use a dependency for many reasons. Some of them may be required to compile and run the projects. There might be others only to run tests (for instance, `junit`). Then there may be dependencies that are required at runtime, say `logback`.

How to do it...

Use the following steps to choose the scope of the dependency:

1. Open the Maven project we had created earlier.

2. Observe the following section:

```
<dependencies>
    <dependency>
      <groupId>junit</groupId>
      <artifactId>junit</artifactId>
      <version>3.8.1</version>
      <scope>test</scope>
    </dependency>
```

3. Remove the preceding lines of code and run the following command:

   `mvn compile`

4. Observe that it runs without any issues.

5. Now, run the following command:

   `mvn test`

6. Note the following error:

   ```
   [INFO] Compiling 1 source file to C:\projects\apache-maven-
   cookbook\project-with
   -dependencies\target\test-classes
   [INFO] -------------------------------------------------------------
   ------
   [ERROR] COMPILATION ERROR:
   [INFO] -------------------------------------------------------------
   ------
   [ERROR] /C:/projects/apache-maven-cookbook/project-with-
   dependencies/src/test/java/com/packt/cookbook/AppTest.java:[3,
   23] package junit.framework does not exist
   ```

How it works...

The Java source code App.java did not have any dependency. Only the source classes were compiled by mvn and thus, the command ran without any error.

The test code AppTest.java required the junit library to build. This is declared in the import statement in the code. The mvn test tried to compile the test classes, and as it did not find the dependency, it failed.

The following information needs to be specified to declare a dependency:

```
<groupId>junit</groupId>
<artifactId>junit</artifactId>
<version>3.8.1</version>
```

The preceding three elements uniquely identify the dependency.

The fourth piece of information is as follows:

```
<scope>test</scope>
```

By default, the scope is compile.

There are six different dependency scopes available:

- compile: This dependency is required for compilation. This automatically means it is required for testing as well as runtime (when the project is run).

- test: This dependency is only required for tests. This means the dependency is typically in the test code. As the test code is not used to run the project, these dependencies are not required for runtime.

- runtime: These dependencies are not required during compilation, but only required to run the project. One example would be the logback dependency if you are using **Simple Logging Facade for Java (slf4j)** to log and want to use logback binding.

- provided: This tells Maven that dependency is required for compilation and runtime, but this dependency need not be packaged with the package for distribution. The dependency will be provided by the user. An example of this dependency is servlet-api. Typically, application servers have these libraries.

- system: This is similar to the provided scope. Here, we need to explicitly provide the location of the JAR file. It is not looked up from the repository. This may be useful to specify a dependency that is not present in the repository:

```
<dependency>
    <groupId>com.myorg</groupId>
    <artifactId>some-jar</artifactId>
    <version>2.0</version>
```

```
    <scope>system</scope>
    <systemPath>${basedir}/lib/some.jar</systemPath>
</dependency>
```

▸ `import`: This is only used on a dependency of the `pom` type in the `dependencyManagement` section. It indicates that the specified pom should be replaced with the dependencies in that pom's `dependencyManagement` section. This is intended to centralize dependencies of large multi-module projects.

See also

▸ The *Manually installing dependencies that are not available in a repository* recipe in this chapter

Getting a report of dependencies

It is useful to get a list of dependencies for a Maven project in order to identify and troubleshoot problems. The Maven Dependency plugin helps us here.

Getting ready

To appreciate this, we need to have a fairly complex project that has several transitive dependencies. You can look at one such project at `https://github.com/selendroid/demoproject-selendroid`.

The project source code is available as a Git repository. A Git repository is typically downloaded by cloning it. To do this, install Git on your system. Refer to the Git setup link (`https://help.github.com/articles/set-up-git/`) for detailed instructions.

How to do it...

Use the following steps, to get a list of dependencies for a Maven project:

1. Clone the open source project `demoproject-selendroid`.

2. Run the following Maven goal:

   `mvn dependency:list`

3. Observe the output as shown in the following screenshot:

```
C:\projects\demoproject-selendroid>mvn dependency:list
[INFO] Scanning for projects...
[INFO]
[INFO] ------------------------------------------------------------------------
[INFO] Building demoproject-selendroid 0.12.0
[INFO] ------------------------------------------------------------------------
[INFO]
[INFO] --- maven-dependency-plugin:2.8:list (default-cli) @ demoproject-selendro
id ---
[INFO]
[INFO] The following files have been resolved:
[INFO]    io.selendroid:selendroid-standalone:jar:0.12.0:compile
[INFO]    io.selendroid:selendroid-server-common:jar:0.12.0:compile
[INFO]    org.seleniumhq.selenium:selenium-java:jar:2.43.1:compile
[INFO]    org.w3c.css:sac:jar:1.3:compile
[INFO]    com.android.tools.ddms:ddmlib:jar:23.0.1:compile
[INFO]    io.selendroid:selendroid-client:jar:0.12.0:compile
[INFO]    xalan:serializer:jar:2.7.1:compile
[INFO]    org.hamcrest:hamcrest-library:jar:1.3:compile
[INFO]    org.tukaani:xz:jar:1.2:compile
[INFO]    io.netty:netty-all:jar:4.0.21.Final:compile
[INFO]    com.google.guava:guava:jar:17.0:compile
[INFO]    net.sourceforge.nekohtml:nekohtml:jar:1.9.21:compile
[INFO]    io.selendroid:android-driver-app:apk:0.12.0:compile
[INFO]    xml-apis:xml-apis:jar:1.4.01:compile
[INFO]    cglib:cglib-nodep:jar:2.1_3:compile
[INFO]    net.sourceforge.htmlunit:htmlunit-core-js:jar:2.15:compile
[INFO]    org.apache.httpcomponents:httpclient:jar:4.3.4:compile
[INFO]    org.apache.httpcomponents:httpcore:jar:4.3.2:compile
[INFO]    org.seleniumhq.selenium:selenium-support:jar:2.43.1:compile
[INFO]    org.hamcrest:hamcrest-core:jar:1.3:compile
[INFO]    net.sf.kxml:kxml2:jar:2.3.0:compile
[INFO]    org.seleniumhq.selenium:selenium-remote-driver:jar:2.43.1:compile
[INFO]    junit:junit:jar:4.8.2:compile
[INFO]    org.eclipse.jetty:jetty-io:jar:8.1.15.v20140411:compile
```

How it works...

The Maven Dependency plugin has several goals to obtain information regarding dependencies as well as manage them.

Interestingly, this goal is not bound to any phase or lifecycle of Maven. This means, when the `mvn dependency:list` command is run, Maven runs the `list` goal and nothing else.

The `dependency:list` parameter tells Maven to run the `list` goal of the Maven Dependency plugin. This analyzes the pom file and generates a list of dependencies for the project.

There's more...

While the dependency list might be good enough for simple cases, a more interesting and useful one would be a dependency report in a tree format.

This can be done by running the `tree` goal of Maven Dependency plugin:

```
mvn dependency:tree
```

Running this on the preceding project gives the following output:

```
C:\projects\demoproject-selendroid>mvn dependency:tree
[INFO] Scanning for projects...
[INFO]
[INFO] ------------------------------------------------------------------------
[INFO] Building demoproject-selendroid 0.12.0
[INFO] ------------------------------------------------------------------------
[INFO]
[INFO] --- maven-dependency-plugin:2.8:tree (default-cli) @ demoproject-selendro
id ---
[INFO] io.selendroid:demoproject-selendroid:jar:0.12.0
[INFO] +- io.selendroid:selendroid-standalone:jar:0.12.0:compile
[INFO] |  +- io.selendroid:selendroid-common:jar:0.12.0:compile
[INFO] |  +- io.selendroid:selendroid-server-common:jar:0.12.0:compile
[INFO] |  |  \- io.netty:netty-all:jar:4.0.21.Final:compile
[INFO] |  +- io.selendroid:selendroid-server:apk:0.12.0:compile
[INFO] |  +- io.selendroid:android-driver-app:apk:0.12.0:compile
[INFO] |  +- org.apache.httpcomponents:httpclient:jar:4.3.4:compile
[INFO] |  |  +- org.apache.httpcomponents:httpcore:jar:4.3.2:compile
[INFO] |  |  +- commons-logging:commons-logging:jar:1.1.3:compile
[INFO] |  |  \- commons-codec:commons-codec:jar:1.6:compile
[INFO] |  +- org.json:json:jar:20090211:compile
[INFO] |  +- commons-io:commons-io:jar:2.2:compile
[INFO] |  +- org.apache.commons:commons-exec:jar:1.1:compile
[INFO] |  +- com.beust:jcommander:jar:1.30:compile
[INFO] |  +- com.android.tools.ddms:ddmlib:jar:23.0.1:compile
[INFO] |  |  +- net.sf.kxml:kxml2:jar:2.3.0:compile
[INFO] |  |  \- com.android.tools:common:jar:23.0.1:compile
[INFO] |  +- org.apache.commons:commons-compress:jar:1.5:compile
[INFO] |  |  \- org.tukaani:xz:jar:1.2:compile
[INFO] |  +- com.google.guava:guava:jar:17.0:compile
[INFO] |  +- org.seleniumhq.selenium:selenium-java:jar:2.43.1:compile
[INFO] |  |  +- org.seleniumhq.selenium:selenium-chrome-driver:jar:2.43.1:compil
e
[INFO] |  |  |  \- org.seleniumhq.selenium:selenium-remote-driver:jar:2.43.1:com
pile
[INFO] |  |  |     +- cglib:cglib-nodep:jar:2.1_3:compile
[INFO] |  |  |     \- org.seleniumhq.selenium:selenium-api:jar:2.43.1:compile
[INFO] |  |  +- org.seleniumhq.selenium:selenium-htmlunit-driver:jar:2.43.1:comp
ile
[INFO] |  |  |  \- net.sourceforge.htmlunit:htmlunit:jar:2.15:compile
[INFO] |  |  |     +- xalan:xalan:jar:2.7.1:compile
[INFO] |  |  |     |  \- xalan:serializer:jar:2.7.1:compile
```

As we can see, this is a better representation of the transitivity of the dependencies. Now we know that which other dependencies are used, for instance, `commons-logging`.

Getting into dependency and avoiding dependency hell

As you use a number of dependencies, each of them in turn may also include further dependencies. A situation may come when there are multiple versions of the same dependencies in the project. This can often lead to errors.

Getting ready

To understand this, we need to have a fairly complex project that has several transitive dependencies. You can look at one such project at `https://github.com/selendroid/demoproject-selendroid`.

Clone the repository on your system. Now, we are ready to see how complex dependencies can get.

How to do it...

Use the following steps to avoid dependency hell:

1. Run the following command:

   ```
   mvn dependency:tree -Dverbose
   ```

2. Note the output as shown in the following screenshot:

```
C:\projects\demoproject-selendroid>mvn dependency:tree -Dverbose
[INFO] Scanning for projects...
[INFO]
[INFO] ------------------------------------------------------------------------
[INFO] Building demoproject-selendroid 0.12.0
[INFO] ------------------------------------------------------------------------
[INFO]
[INFO] --- maven-dependency-plugin:2.8:tree (default-cli) @ demoproject-selendro
id ---
[INFO] io.selendroid:demoproject-selendroid:jar:0.12.0
[INFO] +- io.selendroid:selendroid-standalone:jar:0.12.0:compile
[INFO] |  +- io.selendroid:selendroid-common:jar:0.12.0:compile
[INFO] |  |  \- (org.seleniumhq.selenium:selenium-java:jar:2.43.1:compile - omit
ted for duplicate)
[INFO] |  +- io.selendroid:selendroid-server-common:jar:0.12.0:compile
[INFO] |  |  \- io.netty:netty-all:jar:4.0.21.Final:compile
[INFO] |  +- io.selendroid:selendroid-server:apk:0.12.0:compile
[INFO] |  |  +- (io.selendroid:selendroid-server-common:jar:0.12.0:compile - omi
tted for duplicate)
[INFO] |  |  \- (com.google.code.gson:gson:jar:2.2.1:compile - omitted for dupli
cate)
[INFO] |  +- io.selendroid:android-driver-app:apk:0.12.0:compile
[INFO] |  +- org.apache.httpcomponents:httpclient:jar:4.3.4:compile
[INFO] |  |  +- org.apache.httpcomponents:httpcore:jar:4.3.2:compile
[INFO] |  |  +- commons-logging:commons-logging:jar:1.1.3:compile
[INFO] |  |  \- commons-codec:commons-codec:jar:1.6:compile
[INFO] |  +- org.json:json:jar:20090211:compile
[INFO] |  +- commons-io:commons-io:jar:2.2:compile
[INFO] |  +- org.apache.commons:commons-exec:jar:1.1:compile
[INFO] |  +- com.beust:jcommander:jar:1.30:compile
[INFO] |  +- com.android.tools.ddms:ddmlib:jar:23.0.1:compile
[INFO] |  |  +- net.sf.kxml:kxml2:jar:2.3.0:compile
[INFO] |  |  \- com.android.tools:common:jar:23.0.1:compile
[INFO] |  |      \- (com.google.guava:guava:jar:15.0:compile - omitted for confli
ct with 17.0)
[INFO] |  +- org.apache.commons:commons-compress:jar:1.5:compile
```

How it works...

As you can see, in the course of identifying the dependencies to be used in the project, Maven does a dependency analysis. This reveals two things:

▶ Two or more dependencies require the same version of another dependency. Maven includes a dependency only once.

▶ Two or more dependencies require a different version of another dependency.

Maven resolves this by supporting the *nearest definition*, which means that it will use the version of the dependency closest to your project in the tree of dependencies.

This means it will not necessarily take either the *latest* or the *oldest* version. It will go by the version that it finds *first* in the order of dependencies.

Where the project fails to work due to the incorrect version being used, the correct way to resolve is to explicitly define the desired version of the dependency in your pom file. By the previous strategy, this being the *nearest definition* will get precedence over any other versions defined in any other dependency.

There's more...

Maven provides another way to handle the preceding scenario, namely, by using the dependencyManagement element.

This allows us to directly specify the versions of artifacts to be used when they are encountered in transitive dependencies or in dependencies where no version has been specified. In the example in the preceding section, the guava dependency was directly added to demoproject-selendroid, even though it was not directly used by the project. Instead, demoproject-selendroid can include guava as a dependency in its dependencyManagement section and directly control which version of guava is used when, or if, it is ever referenced.

There is no magic bullet to prevent dependency hell. Even if you manually manage the version of a library that gets included in your project by the preceding mechanism, it does not mean that other transitive dependencies, which depend on a different version of the same library, will suddenly become binary compatible with the managed version.

Downloading dependencies into a folder

Some projects may have a requirement for all the dependencies to be made available, say, in a folder. This could be to archive the dependencies used in a particular version of the build.

How to do it...

Use the following steps to download dependencies in the target/dependency folder:

1. Let us open the demo project that we used in the previous recipe.
2. Run the following command:

    ```
    mvn dependency:copy-dependencies
    ```

3. See the output in the `target/dependency` folder:

```
C:\projects\demoproject-selendroid\target\dependency>dir
 Volume in drive C has no label.
 Volume Serial Number is 04B8-E184

 Directory of C:\projects\demoproject-selendroid\target\dependency

19-02-2015  07:30 PM    <DIR>          .
19-02-2015  07:30 PM    <DIR>          ..
19-02-2015  07:30 PM            33,272 android-driver-app-0.12.0.apk
19-02-2015  07:30 PM           324,238 cglib-nodep-2.1_3.jar
19-02-2015  07:30 PM            82,843 common-23.0.1.jar
19-02-2015  07:30 PM           232,771 commons-codec-1.6.jar
19-02-2015  07:30 PM           575,389 commons-collections-3.2.1.jar
19-02-2015  07:30 PM           256,241 commons-compress-1.5.jar
19-02-2015  07:30 PM            52,543 commons-exec-1.1.jar
19-02-2015  07:30 PM           173,587 commons-io-2.2.jar
19-02-2015  07:30 PM           315,805 commons-lang3-3.1.jar
19-02-2015  07:30 PM            62,050 commons-logging-1.1.3.jar
19-02-2015  07:30 PM           354,647 cssparser-0.9.14.jar
19-02-2015  07:30 PM           267,517 ddmlib-23.0.1.jar
19-02-2015  07:30 PM           189,617 gson-2.2.1.jar
19-02-2015  07:30 PM         2,243,036 guava-17.0.jar
19-02-2015  07:30 PM            45,024 hamcrest-core-1.3.jar
19-02-2015  07:30 PM             4,820 hamcrest-integration-1.3.jar
19-02-2015  07:30 PM            53,070 hamcrest-library-1.3.jar
19-02-2015  07:30 PM         1,452,628 htmlunit-2.15.jar
19-02-2015  07:30 PM         1,026,253 htmlunit-core-js-2.15.jar
19-02-2015  07:30 PM           590,004 httpclient-4.3.4.jar
19-02-2015  07:30 PM           282,269 httpcore-4.3.2.jar
```

How it works...

The `copy-dependencies` goal of the Maven Dependency plugin copies over all the dependencies used in the project, including transitive dependencies, to `target/dependency` folder of the project.

There's more...

This goal takes several parameters to handle various use cases, such as copying pom files of the dependencies, copying parent poms, preserving the folder structure of the repository, and so on.

The folder location can be changed by passing the following argument:

```
mvn dependency:copy-dependencies -DoutputDirectory=dependencies
```

The dependencies will now be copied over to the `dependencies` folder instead of the default `target/dependency` folder.

The folder structure of the repository can be preserved and the poms of the dependencies can be copied over by running the following command:

```
mvn dependency:copy-dependencies -Dmdep.copyPom=true
Dmdep.useRepositoryLayout=true
```

The resultant folder structure will be similar to the repository layout as shown in the following screenshot:

```
C:\projects\demoproject-selendroid\target\dependency>tree /f
Folder PATH listing
Volume serial number is 04B8-E184
C:.
├───cglib
│   └───cglib-nodep
│           maven-metadata-local.xml
│       └───2.1_3
│               cglib-nodep-2.1_3.jar
│               cglib-nodep-2.1_3.pom
│
├───com
│   ├───android
│   │   └───tools
│   │       ├───common
│   │       │       maven-metadata-local.xml
│   │       │   └───23.0.1
│   │       │           common-23.0.1.jar
│   │       │           common-23.0.1.pom
│   │       │
│   │       └───ddms
│   │           └───ddmlib
│   │                   maven-metadata-local.xml
│   │               └───23.0.1
│   │                       ddmlib-23.0.1.jar
│   │                       ddmlib-23.0.1.pom
│   │
│   └───beust
│       └───jcommander
│               maven-metadata-local.xml
│           └───1.30
│                   jcommander-1.30.jar
│                   jcommander-1.30.pom
```

Understanding SNAPSHOT dependencies

In Maven, a SNAPSHOT version is a version of the project/dependency that has not been released. This is indicated by suffixing SNAPSHOT to the version number. Here's an example:

```
<version>1.0-SNAPSHOT</version>
```

You will notice that the project we created using the Maven archetype quickstart had a SNAPSHOT version.

The version number specified before -SNAPSHOT is the version that the released project/dependency is expected to have. So, 1.0-SNAPSHOT indicates 1.0 is not released yet.

As the SNAPSHOT version indicates software under development, Maven deals with these dependencies differently.

How to do it...

One would rarely use the SNAPSHOT version of an external dependency. If you are developing a multi-module project in your organization, chances are you will use SNAPSHOT versions of other modules required in your project.

Let us try the following contrived example:

1. Open one of the projects that we have created.

2. Add the following dependency:

```
<dependency>
    <groupId>org.springframework</groupId>
    <artifactId>spring-context</artifactId>
    <version>4.1.0.BUILD-SNAPSHOT</version>
</dependency>
```

3. Add the following code to specify the repository where the dependency is available:

```
<repositories>
    <repository>
        <id>repository.spring.snapshot</id>
        <name>Spring Snapshot Repository</name>
        <url>http://repo.spring.io/snapshot</url>
    </repository>
</repositories>
```

4. Run the following command:

```
C:\projects\apache-maven-cookbook\project-with-snapshot-
dependencies>mvn verify
```

5. Observe the following results:

```
[INFO] Scanning for projects...

[INFO]

[INFO] --------------------------------------------------------
-----------------

[INFO] Building Project with SNAPSHOT dependencies 1.0-
SNAPSHOT

[INFO] --------------------------------------------------------
-----------------

Downloading:http://repo.spring.io/snapshot/org/springframework
/spring-context/4.1.2.BUILD-SNAPSHOT/maven-metadata.xml

Downloaded:http://repo.spring.io/snapshot/org/springframework/
spring-context/4.1.2.BUILD-SNAPSHOT/maven-metadata.xml (3 KB
at 1.7 KB/sec)
```

```
Downloading:http://repo.spring.io/snapshot/org/springframework
/spring-context/4.1.2.BUILD-SNAPSHOT/spring-context-
4.1.2.BUILD-20141107.161556-92.pom
```

```
Downloaded:http://repo.spring.io/snapshot/org/springframework/
spring-context/4.1.2.BUILD-SNAPSHOT/spring-context-
4.1.2.BUILD-20141107.161556-92.pom (5 KB at 6.8 KB/sec)
```

How it works...

The first thing you would have seen is the need to define a specific repository to download the dependencies. These dependencies are not available in the usual repositories. They reside separately in repositories called **snapshot repositories**. In the preceding example, we specified the snapshot repository where the desired dependencies were available.

The second thing you would notice are the filenames. Each artifact that is being downloaded is appended with `20141107.161556-92`. This is a unique identifier for each `SNAPSHOT` version in the repository. This value changes each time a new `SNAPSHOT` version is available in the repository.

Maven treats `SNAPSHOT` versions differently from release versions.

For a release version, Maven checks if the artifact is available in the local repository that is already downloaded. If so, it does not attempt to fetch the same from the remote repositories.

For `SNAPSHOT` versions, even if the artifact is available locally, it checks the `SNAPSHOT` version for updates in the remote repository based on the update policy that can be configured.

By default, the update interval is once a day. This means, if Maven downloads a `SNAPSHOT` dependency at noon today, it will check for an update to it at noon tomorrow and not before that, irrespective of how many times you build the project.

The update interval can be specified in the repository section of the pom or settings file as follows:

```
<updatePolicy>always<updatePolicy>
```

The choices are `always`, `daily` (default), `interval:X` (where X is an integer in minutes), or `never`. Let's discuss in brief about these choices:

- ▶ `always`: This checks for updates for every Maven run.
- ▶ `daily`: This checks for updates once a day. This does not necessarily mean exactly 24 hours from the last check; just once a day at the start of the day.
- ▶ `interval:X`: This checks for updates after a specified time.

In a multi-module project, it is good to set the `updatePolicy` element value to `always` for intermodule dependencies.

There's more...

As mentioned earlier, there are separate repositories for release and snapshot versions. By default, snapshots are disabled for a release repository and vice versa. The `repository` element has separate `releases` and `snapshots` sub-elements where this can be specified:

```
<repository>
    <id>my-repo</id>
    <name>My Release Repo</name>
    <releases>
      <enabled>true</enabled>
      <updatePolicy>never</updatePolicy>
      <checksumPolicy>fail</checksumPolicy>
    </releases>
    <snapshots>
      <enabled>false</enabled>
      <updatePolicy>always</updatePolicy>
      <checksumPolicy>fail</checksumPolicy>
    </snapshots>
    <url>http://my.repo.url</url>
    <layout>default</layout>
</repository>
```

Typically, for a release repository, `enabled` will be `false` for `snapshots`. For a snapshot repository, `enabled` will be `true` for `snapshots` and `false` for `releases`. This is so that Maven looks at the right repository for the right artifacts and does not unnecessarily look at the wrong repositories each time it needs a dependency.

The `checksumPolicy` element tells Maven what to do in case the checksum of the downloaded dependency does not match the actual checksum. The value of `fail` will stop the build with a checksum error.

Handling dependency download errors

There could be situations when a dependency might not be downloaded due to network problems or other issues. Sometimes, the error reported by Maven might not indicate the problem. It is good to know how to get around this problem.

How to do it...

It is difficult to simulate this problem in a normal scenario, but we can create a contrived scenario, by using the following steps:

1. Modify the dependency version for JUnit in our simple project:

    ```
    <version>3.9.1 </version>
    ```

2. Run the following command:

    mvn verify

3. This will attempt to download the dependency and fail (as the version is invalid):

    ```
    [INFO] Building simple-project 1.0-SNAPSHOT
    [INFO] -------------------------------------------------------
    -----------------
    Downloading:https://repo.maven.apache.org/maven2/junit/junit/3
    .9.1/junit-3.9.1.pom
    [WARNING] The POM for junit:junit:jar:3.9.1 is missing, no
    dependency information available
    Downloading:https://repo.maven.apache.org/maven2/junit/junit/3
    .9.1/junit-3.9.1.jar
    [INFO] -------------------------------------------------------
    -----------------
    [INFO] BUILD FAILURE
    [INFO] -------------------------------------------------------
    -----------------
    [INFO] Total time: 3.329 s
    [INFO] Finished at: 2014-11-08T15:59:33+05:30
    [INFO] Final Memory: 7M/154M
    [INFO] -------------------------------------------------------
    -----------------
    [ERROR] Failed to execute goal on project simple-project:
    Could not resolve dependencies for project
    com.packt.cookbook:simple-project:jar:1.0-SNAPSHOT: Could n
    ot find artifact junit:junit:jar:3.9.1 in central
    (https://repo.maven.apache.org/maven2) -> [Help 1]
    ```

4. Run the command again and observe the results:

```
[ERROR] Failed to execute goal on project simple-project:
Could not resolve dependencies for project
com.packt.cookbook:simple-project:jar:1.0-SNAPSHOT: Failure to
find junit:junit:jar:3.9.1 in
https://repo.maven.apache.org/maven2 was cached in the local
repository, resolution will not be reattempted until the
update interval of central has elapsed or updates are forced -
> [Help 1]
```

5. Delete the folder `3.9.1` (or the files in the folder ending with `.lastUpdated`) in the local repo (`.m2/repository/junit/junit/3.9.1`) and retry.

   The `resolution will not be attempted` error will go away and Maven will attempt to download the dependency again

How it works...

Maven first downloads the pom file of the dependency. It analyzes the pom file and recursively downloads the transitive dependencies specified there. It then downloads the actual dependency file, typically, a JAR file.

When Maven fails to download an artifact, it creates a file with the same name as the artifact it failed to download, but suffixed with `.lastUpdated`. In the file, it puts information related to the download, as shown in the following example:

```
#NOTE: This is an Aether internal implementation file, its format
can be changed without prior notice.
#Sat Nov 08 15:59:33 IST 2014
https\://repo.maven.apache.org/maven2/.lastUpdated=1415442573938
https\://repo.maven.apache.org/maven2/.error=
```

When a request is made to Maven to download the dependency again, maven refers to the contents of this file to decide whether or not maven should reattempt. This is the case for release dependencies. The deletion of this file will ensure maven reattempts to download the dependency when asked.

We have seen how this works for SNAPSHOT dependencies in the *Understanding the SNAPSHOT dependencies* recipe of this chapter.

Detecting unused/undeclared dependencies

As your project becomes large and the number of dependencies increase (including transitive dependencies), it is good to know if we have ended up declaring dependencies that we are not using, or if we are using undeclared dependencies (which are brought in by transitive dependencies).

How to do it...

Use the following steps to detect the unused/undeclared dependencies:

1. Run the following Maven command on the `demo-selendroid` project that we used earlier:

   ```
   mvn dependency:analyze
   ```

2. Note the report generated:

   ```
   [WARNING] Used undeclared dependencies found:
   [WARNING]      org.seleniumhq.selenium:selenium-
   api:jar:2.43.1:compile
   [WARNING]      org.hamcrest:hamcrest-library:jar:1.3:compile
   [WARNING]      io.selendroid:selendroid-
   common:jar:0.12.0:compile
   [WARNING] Unused declared dependencies found:
   [WARNING]      org.hamcrest:hamcrest-integration:jar:1.3:compile
   ```

How it works...

As can be seen from the preceding report, Maven has identified a dependency used by the project that is not declared, for instance the `selenium-api` JAR file. It has also found a dependency that is declared in the pom file, but is not used by the project (`hamcrest-integration`). You could check if the removal causes any side-effect and if not, go ahead.

It is a good practice to explicitly define the dependency used in the project, specifying the version number instead of using it by means of a transitive dependency. This is because we have no control over the version or availability of this transitive dependency.

On the other hand, in order to have better control over dependency conflicts that we saw earlier, it may not be a bad idea to explicitly define versions of dependencies that are not directly required by our project but used by our dependencies.

Manually installing dependencies that are not available in a repository

There may be situations where a library, which is not present in any Maven repository, needs to be used. We have seen one way to use it, that is, specifying it as a dependency with `system` scope and explicitly specifying the path to it.

The problem with this approach is that this dependency will not be available if you need to distribute your project as a library.

Maven provides a mechanism to install an artifact to your local repository so that you can declare and use it like other dependencies.

How to do it...

Use the following steps to manually install the dependencies that aren't available in a repository:

1. Add the following dependency to the simple project that we created earlier:

   ```
   <dependency>
           <groupId>org.apache.tomcat</groupId>
           <artifactId>apache-tomcat</artifactId>
           <version>8.0.14</version>
           <type>tar.gz</type>
           </dependency>
   ```

   The project will fail to compile with the error of a missing dependency

2. Now run the following Maven command:

   ```
   C:\projects\apache-maven-cookbook\project-with-dependency-not-
   in-repo>mvn install:install-file -DgroupId=org.apache.tomcat -
   DartifactId=apache-tomcat -Dversion=8.0.14 -Dpackaging=tar.gz
   -Dfile=C:\Users\raghu\Downloads\apache-tomcat-8.0.14.tar.gz -
   DgeneratePom=true
   ```

3. Note the result:

   ```
   [INFO] --- maven-install-plugin:2.4:install-file (default-cli)
   @ project-with-dependency-not-in-repo ---
   ```

   ```
   [INFO] Installing C:\Users\raghu\Downloads\apache-tomcat-
   8.0.14.tar.gz to C:\software\maven\org\apache\tomcat\apache-
   tomcat\8.0.14\apache-tomcat-8.0.14.tar.gz
   ```

```
[INFO] Installing
C:\Users\raghu\AppData\Local\Temp\mvninstall182957602718131623 9
5.pom to C:\software\maven\org\apache\tomcat\apache-
tomcat\8.0.14\apache-tomcat-8.0.14.pom
```

How it works...

The `install-file` goal of the Maven Install plugin allows dependencies to be installed to the local repository. It takes `groupId`, `artifactId`, `version`, and `packaging` type as parameters so that it can place the dependency suitably in the repository as well as create a simple pom file for it.

This method is not ideal in a project with multiple developers, as each developer needs to perform this step manually. One way to deal with this is to install this dependency in a repository manager that is used by the organization. As the developers will be using this repository manager as a `mirror`, Maven will find the dependency from the `mirror` and proceed.

In such a case, we could use the `deploy` goal of the Maven deploy plugin to install the artifact to the remote repository.

Some remote repositories have access control. Maven allows access details to be specified in the `server` element. It is best to specify this in `settings.xml` as this file is specific to each user.

There's more...

Projects with dependencies that are installed by this method are again not distributable, as those using them will fail to find the dependencies.

Where projects are expected to be distributed and included by others as dependencies, a different approach needs to be followed—the static **in-project repository** solution. Use the following steps to follow the in-project repository approach:

1. Create a repository inside your project by adding the following in your pom file:

    ```
    <repository>
        <id>in-project-repo</id>
        <releases>
            <checksumPolicy>ignore</checksumPolicy>
        </releases>
        <url>file://${project.basedir}/lib</url>
    </repository>
    ```

2. Use the following command to install the dependency to this repository:

```
mvn install:install-file -DgroupId=org.apache.tomcat -
DartifactId=apache-tomcat -Dversion=8.0.14 -Dpackaging=tar.gz
-Dfile=C:\Users\raghu\Downloads\apache-tomcat-8.0.14.tar.gz -
DgeneratePom=true -DlocalRepositoryPath=lib
```

What have we achieved? Now, the dependency is packaged along with the source code in the `lib` folder of our project and available for distribution. This is transparent to the user as they do not need to do anything special to access it.

Dependency management using Eclipse

We have seen that the Eclipse IDE provides support for Maven projects and allows us to run Maven commands from the IDE. Let us now see how we can manage dependencies using Eclipse.

How to do it...

Use the following steps in Eclipse IDE to manage the dependencies:

1. Open the demoproject-selendroid file in Eclipse.

2. Open the `pom.xml` file.

3. Click on the **Dependencies** tab as shown in the following screenshot:

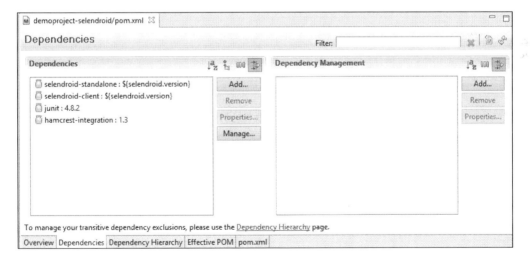

4. A new dependency can be added by clicking on the **Add...** button (see in the preceding screenshot for the **Add...** button):

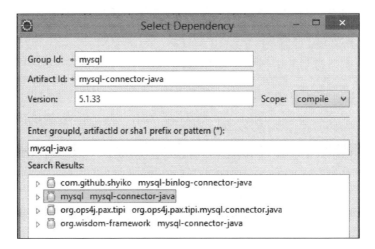

As you can see in the preceding screenshot, you can specify the values in the **Group Id:**, **Artifact Id:**, and **Version:** textboxes along with the value in the **Scope** dropdown. Alternately, you can search for an artifact in the **Enter groupId, artifactId or sha1 prefix or pattern (*):** textbox, and eclipse will populate the relevant columns based on your selection in the **Search Results** list.

5. You can also see the dependency tree by clicking on the **Dependency Hierarchy** tab:

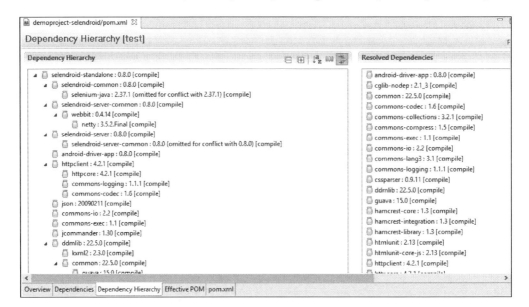

How it works...

As Eclipse has built-in support for Maven, it allows visualization of dependencies by parsing the pom file. It also calls various Maven commands (such as `dependency:tree`) internally to build the hierarchy and display the same.

There's more...

We saw that users can search for and add dependencies. For this to work, navigate to **Windows | Preferences | Maven** and check the **Download repository index updates on startup** option to download indexes, as shown in the following screenshot:

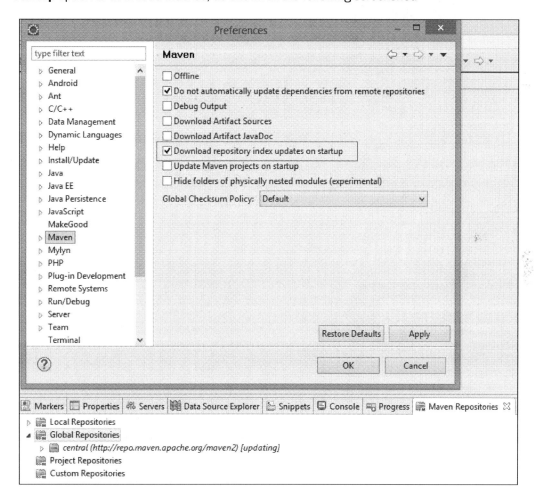

You may need to restart Eclipse for this to take effect. Also, you can enable the **Maven Repositories** view (see in the preceding screenshot), see the repositories, and also update the index as required.

Dependency management using NetBeans

Like Eclipse, NetBeans also allows dependencies to be managed and viewed through the IDE. Unlike Eclipse, NetBeans displays a graphical view of the dependencies along with additional information, which makes it easy for developers to troubleshoot issues.

How to do it...

Use the following steps in the NetBeans IDE to manage the dependencies:

1. Open the `demoproject-selendroid` file in NetBeans.

2. Open the `pom.xml` file.

3. Click on the **Graph** tab:

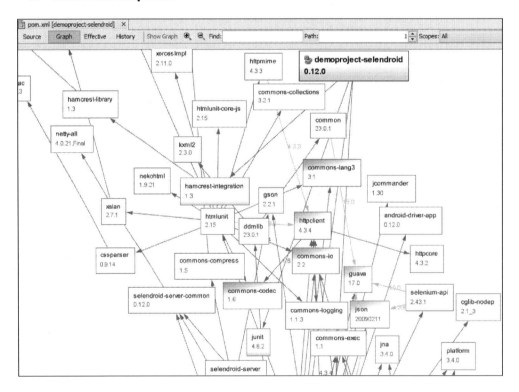

4. Hover over one of the dependencies in red (**commons-codec**):

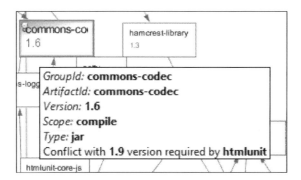

5. Hover over one of the dependencies in orange (**httpclient**):

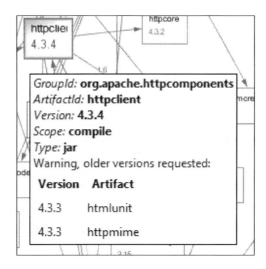

How it works...

NetBeans creates a graph of all the project dependencies and displays the same. It colors the dependencies that have conflicts in red and those that have warnings in orange. On hovering, NetBeans displays details of the issues.

This allows the user to take suitable action.

Dependency management using IntelliJ IDEA

Unlike Eclipse and NetBeans, viewing dependencies as graphs is only possible in the IntelliJ IDEA Ultimate version, which is commercial. The Community Edition does not support this option.

How to do it...

Use the following steps in IntelliJ Idea Ultimate version to manage the dependencies:

1. Open the `demoproject-selendroid` file in the IntelliJ IDEA Ultimate edition.

2. Right-click on the `pom.xml` file.

3. Click on the **Show Dependencies...** option (See this option in the preceding screenshot) and observe the following screenshot:

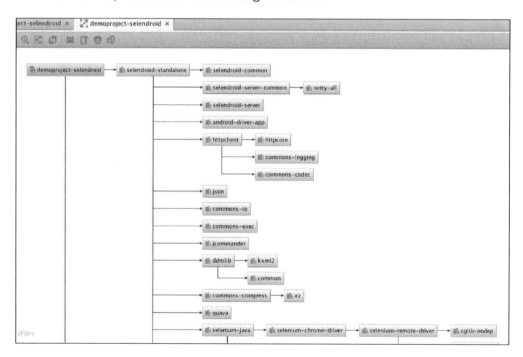

How it works...

IntelliJ IDEA has first-class support for Maven projects. It reads the `pom.xml` file of the project, parses it, and identifies all the dependencies, including transitive dependencies. It then displays the same in a graphical manner, allowing users to visualize the project.

6
Code Quality Plugins

In this chapter, we will review some of the available tools for the Java language and how to use them in the context of Maven. We will cover the following recipes:

- Analyzing code coverage with the Maven JaCoCo plugin
- Analyzing code coverage with the Maven Cobertura plugin
- Analyzing code with the Maven PMD plugin
- Analyzing code with the Maven Checkstyle plugin
- Analyzing code with the Maven FindBugs plugin
- Generating source references with the Maven JXR plugin
- Analyzing code with the Maven SonarQube plugin

Introduction

It is one thing to write code and another to write good code. The subjectivity of code quality is greatly reduced by having coding guidelines/standards. Whether a developer follows coding standards or not can be verified by subjecting the code to a code review. On the other hand, there are tools that automatically perform these reviews against defined standards.

In addition to code quality, programming best practices also recommend writing automated unit tests for the code. The line and branch coverage achieved by these unit tests can also be quantitatively measured by tools.

Analyzing code coverage with the Maven JaCoCo plugin

JaCoCo is a free Java code coverage tool. This is essentially the successor to Emma, and it has been developed by the EclEmma team as an Eclipse project.

JaCoCo offers line and branch coverage.

Getting ready

Maven is set up on your system and is verified to work. To do this, refer to the first three recipes of *Chapter1, Getting Started*.

How to do it...

Use the following steps to analyze the code coverage with the Maven JaCoCo plugin:

1. Open the pom file of a project that has unit tests (for instance, `project-with-tests`).

2. Add the following code:

```
<plugin>
  <groupId>org.jacoco</groupId>
  <artifactId>jacoco-maven-plugin</artifactId>
  <version>0.7.2.201409121644</version>
  <executions>
    <execution>
      <id>default-prepare-agent</id>
      <goals>
        <goal>prepare-agent</goal>
      </goals>
    </execution>
    <execution>
      <id>default-report</id>
      <phase>prepare-package</phase>
      <goals>
        <goal>report</goal>
      </goals>
    </execution>
  </executions>
</plugin>
```

3. Run the following command from the command prompt:

```
mvn package
```

4. Note the output for the preceding command:

```
[INFO] --- jacoco-maven-plugin:0.7.2.201409121644:prepare-
agent (default-prepare-agent) @ project-with-tests ---
```

```
[INFO] argLine set to -
javaagent:C:\\software\\maven\\org\\jacoco\\org.jacoco.ag
ent\\0.7.2.201409121644\\org.jacoco.agent-0.7.2.201409121644-
runtime.jar=destfile=C:\\projects\\apache-maven-
cookbook\\project-with-tests\\target\\jacoco.exec
```

```
[INFO] --- jacoco-maven-plugin:0.7.2.201409121644:report
(default-report) @ project-with-tests ---
```

```
[INFO] Analyzed bundle 'Project with Tests with 1 classes
```

5. Open the `index.html` file generated in the `target/site/jacoco` folder:

Element	Missed Instructions ⬦	Cov. ⬦	Missed Branches ⬦	Cov. ⬦	Missed ⬦	Cxty ⬦	Missed ⬦	Lines ⬦	Missed ⬦
⊞ com.packt.cookbook		37%		n/a	3	5	3	5	3
Total	12 of 19	37%	0 of 0	n/a	3	5	3	5	3

Created with JaCoCo 0.7.2.201409121644

How it works...

In the pom file, we instruct Maven to run the following two goals of the Maven JaCoCo plugin:

▸ `prepare-agent`: This is bound by default to the `initialize` phase of the Maven default lifecycle. The goal runs and prepares the agent that does the analysis.

▸ `report`: This agent gathers test coverage information when the tests are run and creates the report as part of the prepare-package phase (which we have explicitly specified).

The report gives information about the test coverage. Green indicates lines that are covered by tests and red indicates lines that are not covered by tests. In the preceding example, **12 of 19** instructions are not covered by tests.

There's more...

You could subject the project to code coverage and generate the same report without making any changes to the pom file. To do this, run the following command:

```
mvn jacoco:prepare-agent test jacoco:report
```

Now, you may get the following error:

```
[ERROR] No plugin found for prefix 'jacoco' in the current project
and in the plugin groups [org.apache.maven.plugins] available from
the repositories [local (C:\software\maven), central
(https://repo.maven.apache.org/maven2)] -> [Help 1]
```

To fix this, specify the `groupId` and `artifactId` parameters of the plugin explicitly. In the *Configuring Maven to search for plugins* recipe of *Chapter 8, Handling Typical Build Requirements*, we will see an alternate way to address this.

In the following code, what what we will be doing is explicitly calling the relevant goals that we saw getting executed earlier. So, first `prepare-agent` will run, followed by `test`, and then the `report` goal:

```
mvn org.jacoco:jacoco-maven-plugin:prepare-agent test
org.jacoco:jacoco-maven-plugin:report
```

How about failing the build if the code coverage is below a threshold value? To do this, perform the following steps:

1. Add the following execution block to the plugin configuration in the `build` section specified earlier:

```
<execution>
    <id>default-check</id>
    <phase>prepare-package</phase>
    <goals>
        <goal>check</goal>
    </goals>
    <configuration>
        <rules>
            <rule>
                <element>BUNDLE</element>
                <limits>
                    <limit>
                        <counter>COMPLEXITY</counter>
                        <value>COVEREDRATIO</value>
                        <minimum>0.60</minimum>
                    </limit>
```

```
                  </limits>
               </rule>
            </rules>
         </configuration>
      </execution>
```

2. Run the following command:

   mvn package

3. Observe the result as shown in following screenshot:

```
[INFO] --- jacoco-maven-plugin:0.7.2.201409121644:report (default-report) @ proj
ect-with-tests ---
[INFO] Analyzed bundle 'Project with Tests' with 1 classes
[INFO]
[INFO] --- jacoco-maven-plugin:0.7.2.201409121644:check (default-check) @ projec
t-with-tests ---
[INFO] Analyzed bundle 'Project with Tests' with 1 classes
[WARNING] Rule violated for bundle Project with Tests: complexity covered ratio
is 0.40, but expected minimum is 0.60
[INFO] ------------------------------------------------------------------------
[INFO] BUILD FAILURE
[INFO] ------------------------------------------------------------------------
[INFO] Total time: 3.486 s
[INFO] Finished at: 2014-11-15T22:23:37+05:30
[INFO] Final Memory: 16M/223M
[INFO] ------------------------------------------------------------------------
[ERROR] Failed to execute goal org.jacoco:jacoco-maven-plugin:0.7.2.201409121644
:check (default-check) on project project-with-tests: Coverage checks have not b
een met. See log for details. -> [Help 1]
```

Analyzing code coverage with the Maven Cobertura plugin

Cobertura is another popular Java tool that calculates the percentage of code accessed by tests. It is based on **jcoverage**. There are many ways to use Cobertura, including standalone, through Ant script, and Maven. Let us use the Maven Cobertura plugin.

How to do it...

Use the following steps to analyze the code coverage with the Maven Cobertura plugin:

1. Open a Maven project that has unit tests (for instance, project-with-tests).

2. Run the following command:

   mvn cobertura:cobertura

3. Observe the following output:

   ```
   [INFO] <<< cobertura-maven-plugin:2.6:cobertura (default-cli)
   < [cobertura]test@ project-with-tests <<<

   [INFO]
   ```

```
[INFO] --- cobertura-maven-plugin:2.6:cobertura (default-cli)
@ project-with-tests ---

[INFO] Cobertura 2.0.3 - GNU GPL License (NO WARRANTY) - See
COPYRIGHT file

Report time: 165ms

[ERROR] Nov 15, 2014 5:06:25 PM

net.sourceforge.cobertura.coveragedata.CoverageDataFileHand
ler loadCoverageData

INFO: Cobertura: Loaded information on 1 classes.
```

4. See the report generated:

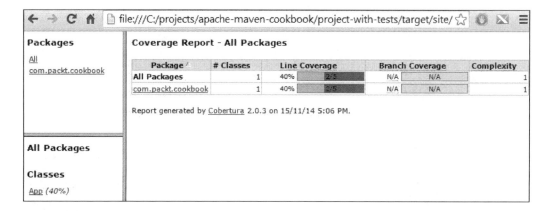

How it works...

JaCoCo instruments the code online when the tests are running and hence, it needs to have the agent running. On the other hand, Cobertura instruments the bytecode during compilation offline. The `cobertura` goal of the Cobertura Maven plugin instruments the project, runs the tests, and generates the report.

There are separate goals to `instrument` and `check` results, if required.

There's more...

What if we want to fail the build if the code coverage is below a threshold level? We can set up Cobertura to do this:

1. Add the following to the pom file:

```
<plugin>
    <groupId>org.codehaus.mojo</groupId>
    <artifactId>cobertura-maven-plugin</artifactId>
```

```xml
<version>2.6</version>
<configuration>
  <check>
    <branchRate>85</branchRate>
    <lineRate>85</lineRate>
    <haltOnFailure>true</haltOnFailure>
  </check>
</configuration>
<executions>
  <execution>
    <goals>
      <goal>check</goal>
    </goals>
  </execution>
</executions>
</plugin>
```

2. Run the following command:

    mvn cobertura:check

3. Observe the output as shown in the following screenshot:

```
[INFO] <<< cobertura-maven-plugin:2.6:check (default-cli) < [cobertura]test @ pr
)ject-with-tests <<<
[INFO]
[INFO] --- cobertura-maven-plugin:2.6:check (default-cli) @ project-with-tests -
[INFO] Cobertura 2.0.3 - GNU GPL License (NO WARRANTY) - See COPYRIGHT file

[ERROR] Nov 15, 2014 5:27:22 PM net.sourceforge.cobertura.coveragedata.CoverageD
ataFileHandler loadCoverageData
INFO: Cobertura: Loaded information on 1 classes.
:om.packt.cookbook.App failed check. Line coverage rate of 40.0% is below 85.0%

[INFO] ------------------------------------------------------------------------
[INFO] BUILD FAILURE
[INFO] ------------------------------------------------------------------------
[INFO] Total time: 8.179 s
[INFO] Finished at: 2014-11-15T17:27:22+05:30
[INFO] Final Memory: 9M/157M
[INFO] ------------------------------------------------------------------------
[ERROR] Failed to execute goal org.codehaus.mojo:cobertura-maven-plugin:2.6:chec
k (default-cli) on project project-with-tests: Coverage check failed. See messag
es above. -> [Help 1]
```

The build has failed because, in the pom file, we specified that the build should be halted if the coverage is less than 85%.

Analyzing code with the Maven PMD plugin

PMD is a source code analyzer. It finds common programming flaws such as unused variables, empty catch blocks, and unnecessary object creation. It also includes the **Copy/Paste Detector** (**CPD**) that finds duplicated code.

How to do it...

Use the following steps to run PMD on a Maven project:

1. Open the Maven project for which you want to do a PMD analysis (for instance, `project-with-violations`).

2. Run the following command:

   mvn pmd:pmd pmd:cpd

3. Observe the output:

   ```
   [INFO] --- maven-pmd-plugin:3.2:pmd (default-cli) @ project-
   with-violations ---

   [WARNING] Unable to locate Source XRef to link to - DISABLED

   [INFO] --- maven-pmd-plugin:3.2:cpd (default-cli) @ project-
   with-violations ---

   [WARNING] Unable to locate Source XRef to link to - DISABLED

   [INFO] ------------------------------------------------------
   -----------------

   [INFO] BUILD SUCCESS
   ```

4. Check the contents of the `target` folder:

   ```
   C:\projects\apache-maven-cookbook\project-with-violations\target>tree /f
   Folder PATH listing
   Volume serial number is 04B8-E184
   C:.
       cpd.xml
       java-basic.xml
       java-imports.xml
       java-unusedcode.xml
       pmd.xml

   └───site
           cpd.html
           pmd.html
   ```

5. Open the `pmd.xml` report:

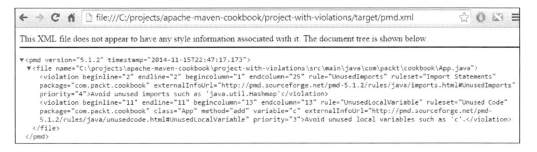

6. Open the `cpd.html` file in the `site` folder:

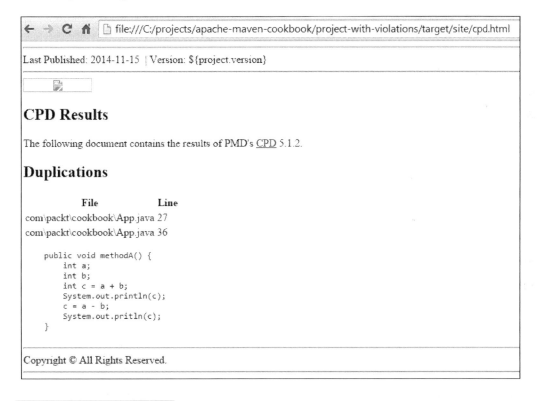

How it works...

The `pmd` or `cpd` goals of the Maven PMD plugin are not bound to any phase. Also, they analyze the Java source and thus, do not need any other Maven phase or goal to be run.

When the `pmd` goal is run, it generates a PMD site report using default rulesets and the configuration set in the plugin. It also generates a pmd output file in the XML format.

You can also define your own customized ruleset. To do this, add the following code in the `configuration` section of the pom file:

```
<reporting>
    <plugins>
      <plugin>
        <groupId>org.apache.maven.plugins</groupId>
        <artifactId>maven-pmd-plugin</artifactId>
        <version>3.4</version>
        <configuration>
          <rulesets>
            <!-- Two rule sets that come bundled with PMD -->
            <ruleset>/rulesets/java/braces.xml</ruleset>
            <ruleset>/rulesets/java/naming.xml</ruleset>
            <!-- Custom local file system rule set -->
            <ruleset>d:\rulesets\strings.xml</ruleset>
            <!-- Custom remote rule set accessed via a URL -->
            <ruleset>http://localhost/design.xml</ruleset>
          </rulesets>
        </configuration>
      </plugin>
    </plugins>
</reporting>
```

Likewise, when the `cpd` goal is run, it generates a similar report for duplicated code. By default, the minimum token count that it considers to report that code is duplicated is 100 tokens (which is typically 10 lines of code).

There's more...

The plugin can be made to fail the build by using the check goal in the following way:

1. Add the following code to the pom file of `project-with-violations`:

```
<build>
  <plugins>
    <plugin>
      <groupId>org.apache.maven.plugins</groupId>
      <artifactId>maven-pmd-plugin</artifactId>
      <version>3.4</version>
      <executions>
        <execution>
          <goals>
            <goal>check</goal>
```

```
            <goal>cpd-check</goal>
          </goals>
        </execution>
      </executions>
    </plugin>
  </plugins>
</build>
```

2. Run the following command:

    mvn verify

3. Observe the output as shown in the following screenshot:

```
[INFO]
[INFO] --- maven-pmd-plugin:3.2:check (default-cli) @ project-with-violations ---
[INFO] -----------------------------------------------------------------------
[INFO] BUILD FAILURE
[INFO] -----------------------------------------------------------------------
[INFO] Total time: 2.878 s
[INFO] Finished at: 2014-11-15T22:59:02+05:30
[INFO] Final Memory: 20M/226M
[INFO] -----------------------------------------------------------------------
[ERROR] Failed to execute goal org.apache.maven.plugins:maven-pmd-plugin:3.2:che
ck (default-cli) on project project-with-violations: You have 2 PMD violations.
For more details see:C:\projects\apache-maven-cookbook\project-with-violations\t
arget\pmd.xml -> [Help 1]
```

Analyzing code with the Maven Checkstyle plugin

Checkstyle is a tool that helps programmers follow coding standards. It automates the process of checking if defined coding standards are followed. It can support any coding standards by suitable configuration. Like other tools, it can be run standalone as well as integrated with Maven.

How to do it...

Use the following steps to analyze code with the Maven Checkstyle plugin:

1. Open the Maven project for which you want to do a Checkstyle analysis (for instance, project-with-violations).

2. Run the following command:

    mvn checkstyle:checkstyle

3. Observe the output as shown in the following screenshot:

```
[INFO]

[INFO] --- maven-checkstyle-plugin:2.13:checkstyle (default-
cli) @ project-with-violations ---

[INFO]

[INFO] There are 29 checkstyle errors.

[WARNING] Unable to locate Source XRef to link to - DISABLED

[INFO] -------------------------------------------------------
-----------------

[INFO] BUILD SUCCESS
```

4. Open the `checkstyle-result.xml` report in the `target` folder:

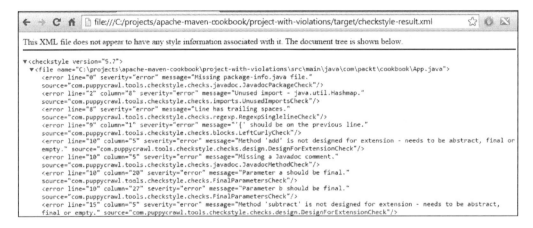

How it works...

Unlike the `pmd`, `checkstyle` goal of Maven, the Checkstyle plugin is not bound to any phase.

When the `checkstyle` goal is run, it generates a Checkstyle site report using default rulesets and the configuration set in the plugin. It also generates a Checkstyle output file in the XML format.

The Maven Checkstyle plugin supports several configuration options to customize the rules, exclude files from being checked, and so on. Let's briefly discuss the examples that show usage of Maven Checkstyle plugin in some advanced usecases:

1. Checkstyle rules can be specified inline in the `configuration` section of the plugin:

```
<configuration>
  <checkstyleRules>
    <module name="Checker">
      <module name="TreeWalker">
        <module name="FinalLocalVariable">
          <property name="tokens" value="VARIABLE_DEF,PARAMETER_
DEF"/>
        </module>
      </module>
    </module>
  </checkstyleRules>
</configuration>
```

2. They can also be specified in an external file and referred using the `configLocation` element:

```
<plugin>
  <groupId>org.apache.maven.plugins</groupId>
  <artifactId>maven-checkstyle-plugin</artifactId>
  <version>2.14</version>
  <configuration>
    <configLocation>checkstyle.xml</configLocation>
  </configuration>
</plugin>
```

3. A Suppressions filter can be created to tell Checkstyle not to report violations on specific files and specific sections of the files:

```
<suppressions>
  <suppress checks="JavadocStyleCheck"
            files="GeneratedObject.java"
            lines="50-9999"/>
  <suppress checks="MagicNumberCheck"
            files="LegacyDatasetConvertor.java"
            lines="221,250-295"/>
</suppressions>
```

There's more...

As in the case of PMD, we can configure the Maven Checkstyle plugin such that it fails a build in case of errors:

1. Add the following code to the pom file of `project-with-violations`:

```
<build>
    <plugins>
      <plugin>
        <groupId>org.apache.maven.plugins</groupId>
        <artifactId>maven-checkstyle-plugin</artifactId>
        <version>2.14</version>
        <executions>
          <execution>
            <id>verify-style</id>
            <phase>process-sources</phase>
            <goals>
              <goal>check</goal>
            </goals>
          </execution>
        </executions>
      </plugin>
    </plugins>
  </build>
```

2. Run the following Maven command:

   `mvn verify`

3. Observe the output as shown in the following screenshot:

Analyzing code with the Maven FindBugs plugin

FindBugs is another tool that uses static analysis to inspect Java bytecode for bugs in a Java code. It is based on the concept of bug patterns. A bug pattern is a code snippet that is often an error.

How to do it...

Let us see how we can use the Maven FindBugs plugin to analyze and identify defects in our code:

1. Open the Maven project for which you want to do the FindBugs analysis.

2. Run the following command:

   ```
   mvn clean compile findbugs:findbugs
   ```

3. Observe the output:

   ```
   [INFO] --- maven-compiler-plugin:3.1:compile (default-compile)
   @ project-with-violations ---

   [INFO] Changes detected - recompiling the module!

   [INFO] Compiling 1 source file to C:\projects\apache-maven
   cookbook\project-with-violations\target\classes

   [INFO]

   [INFO] --- findbugs-maven-plugin:3.0.0:findbugs (default-cli)
   @ project-with-violations ---

   [INFO] Fork Value is true

   [java] Warnings generated: 3

   [INFO] Done FindBugs Analysis....
   ```

4. Open the generated XML file `findbugsXml.xml` in the `target` folder:

How it works...

When the `findbugs` goal of the FindBugs plugin is run, it analyzes the bytecode and reports errors to an output file in the XML format. Unlike Checkstyle and the PMD plugins, it does not generate a default site report unless configured differently.

> As FindBugs works on bytecode, the project needs to be compiled before the FindBugs analysis can be run. Otherwise, you will not find any FindBugs defects!

FindBugs also provides several options that allow you to specify the classes to be included/excluded from analysis, specify the rules to be run, and to fail when errors crop up during the build. Let's briefly discuss some examples that describe the basic usage of the FindBugs plugin:

* Filter bugs to report: This plugin allows us to specify classes and methods that can be included or excluded from reporting:

```
<plugin>
    <groupId>org.codehaus.mojo</groupId>
    <artifactId>findbugs-maven-plugin</artifactId>
    <version>3.0.1-SNAPSHOT</version>
    <configuration>
        <excludeFilterFile>findbugs
        exclude.xml</excludeFilterFile>
        <includeFilterFile>findbugs-
        include.xml</includeFilterFile>
```

```
        </configuration>
    </plugin>
```

▶ Bug detectors to run: We can also specify which detectors to run. This can be done in the following manner:

```
<plugin>
    <groupId>org.codehaus.mojo</groupId>
    <artifactId>findbugs-maven-plugin</artifactId>
    <version>3.0.1-SNAPSHOT</version>
    <configuration>
<visitors>FindDeadLocalStores,UnreadFields</visitors>
    </configuration>
</plugin>
```

There's more...

You can also launch the FindBugs GUI to view the report in a graphical format:

1. To do this, run the following Maven command:

    mvn compile findbugs:findbugs findbugs:gui

2. Observe the FindBugs screen:

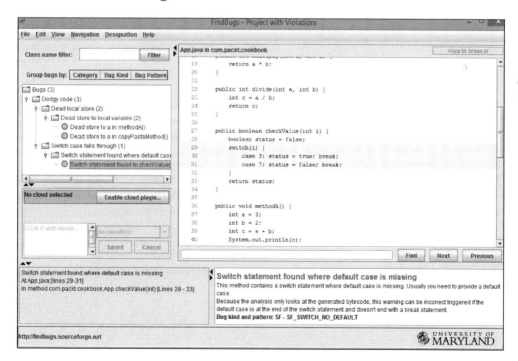

Generating source references with the Maven JXR plugin

You may have observed the following warnings when running the PMD or Checkstyle plugin:

```
[INFO] --- maven-pmd-plugin:3.2:pmd (default-cli) @ project-with-
violations ---

[WARNING] Unable to locate Source XRef to link to - DISABLED

[INFO] --- maven-checkstyle-plugin:2.13:checkstyle (default-cli) @
project-with-violations ---

[INFO]

[INFO] There are 36 checkstyle errors.

[WARNING] Unable to locate Source XRef to link to - DISABLED
```

The plugins attempt to link the violation to the specific lines in the cross-reference of the source. As they are unable to find this cross-reference, they display the warning.

To generate this cross-reference, we need to use the Maven JXR plugin.

How to do it...

Use the following steps to generate source references with the Maven JXR plugin:

1. Open the project for which you want to run the cross-reference.

2. Run the following Maven command:

   ```
   mvn jxr:jxr
   ```

3. Observe the output:

   ```
   [INFO]

   [INFO] --- maven-jxr-plugin:2.5:jxr (default-cli) @ project-
   with-violations ---

   [INFO] -----------------------------------------------------------
   ----------------
   ```

4. Browse the `target/site` folder.

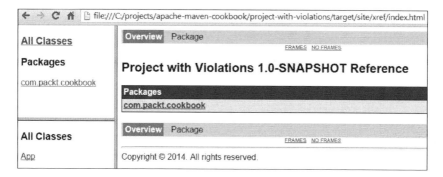

5. Open the contents of the `xref` folder in the browser:

How it works...

When the `jxr` goal of the Maven JXR plugin is run, it generates a cross-reference of all the source files of the project. The format is similar to Javadoc, but on clicking on the class, you get to see the source code with the line numbers:

There's more...

Once the cross-reference exists, code quality tools, such as PMD and Checkstyle, link to this reference automatically by using the following steps:

1. Run the following Maven command:

   ```
   mvn jxr:jxr checkstyle:checkstyle
   ```

2. Open the Checkstyle report in the browser:

Severity Category	Rule	Message	Line
Error javadoc	JavadocPackage	Missing package-info.java file.	
Error regexp	RegexpSingleline	Line has trailing spaces.	7
Error blocks	LeftCurly	'{' should be on the previous line.	8
Error design	DesignForExtension	Method 'add' is not designed for extension - needs to be abstract, final or empty.	9
Error javadoc	JavadocMethod	Missing a Javadoc comment.	9
Error misc	FinalParameters	Parameter a should be final.	9
Error misc	FinalParameters	Parameter b should be final.	9
Error design	DesignForExtension	Method 'subtract' is not designed for extension - needs to be abstract, final or empty.	14
Error javadoc	JavadocMethod	Missing a Javadoc comment.	14
Error misc	FinalParameters	Parameter a should be final.	14

You can now see the line numbers against each of the violations, with the link to the line number in the cross-referenced source code.

Analyzing code with the Maven SonarQube plugin

Each of the code analysis tools we have seen in the previous sections identify specific issues in the code. While Checkstyle looks for violations in coding guidelines, PMD identifies common coding errors, and FindBugs detects bug patterns.

You could have your project configured to run all the three. In addition, you could also run plugins to identify coverage. You could also do all these and more by doing a SonarQube analysis of the project.

SonarQube is a platform to manage code quality. It is a web-based application, where rules, alerts, thresholds, and other metrics can be configured. It provides various ways to analyze code. The results of the analysis can then be viewed in a web application. SonarQube also provides several paid plugins, such as **SQALE**, and for specific languages, such as Cobol and C++.

Getting ready...

Let's briefly discuss some basic requirements for using the Maven SonarQube plugin:

1. Visit the download page for SonarQube at `http://www.sonarqube.org/downloads/`.

2. Download the latest release.

3. Unzip the ZIP file to a folder of your choice.

4. Based on the platform, start the server by following the instructions.

5. Confirm that the server is running by visiting the web page at `http://localhost:9000/` (assuming it's a default installation).

How to do it...

Use the following steps to analyze the code with the Maven SonarQube plugin:

1. Open the Maven project for which you want to do SonarQube analysis.

2. Run the following Maven command:

    mvn sonar:sonar

3. Observe the output as shown in the following screenshot:

```
[INFO] ---- sonar-maven-plugin:2.4:sonar (default-cli) @ project-with-violations
[INFO] SonarQube version: 4.1.2
INFO: Default locale: "en_IN", source code encoding: "UTF-8"
INFO: Work directory: C:\projects\apache-maven-cookbook\project-with-violations\
target\sonar
INFO: SonarQube Server 4.1.2
[INFO] [06:04:02.681] Load batch settings
[INFO] [06:04:02.962] User cache: C:\Users\raghu\.sonar\cache
[INFO] [06:04:02.962] Install plugins
[INFO] [06:04:03.571] Install JDBC driver
[WARN] [06:04:03.587] H2 database should be used for evaluation purpose only
[INFO] [06:04:03.587] Create JDBC datasource for jdbc:h2:tcp://localhost/sonar
[INFO] [06:04:04.728] Initializing Hibernate
[INFO] [06:04:07.869] Load project settings
[INFO] [06:04:07.994] Apply project exclusions
[INFO] [06:04:08.150] ------------- Scan Project with Violations
[INFO] [06:04:08.150] Load module settings
[INFO] [06:04:08.730] Quality profile : [name=Sonar way,language=java]
[INFO] [06:04:08.761] Excluded tests:
[INFO] [06:04:08.761]    **/package-info.java
[INFO] [06:04:08.839] Index files
[INFO] [06:04:08.870] 2 files indexed
[INFO] [06:04:08.995] Loading technical debt model...
[INFO] [06:04:09.419] Loading technical debt model done: 424 ms
[INFO] [06:04:09.450] Configure Maven plugins
[INFO] [06:04:09.638] Compare to previous analysis (2014-11-20)
[INFO] [06:04:09.685] Compare over 30 days (2014-10-22, analysis of 2014-11-20 0
6:58:58.441)
[INFO] [06:04:09.903] JaCoCo agent (version 0.6.3.201306030806) extracted: C:\Us
ers\raghu\AppData\Local\Temp\jacocoagent1846567220462860263.jar
```

4. Visit the Sonar web page at `http://localhost:9000`:

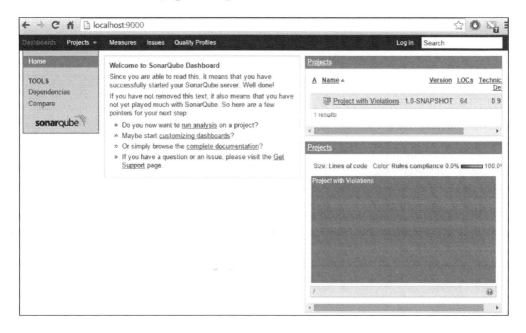

5. Click on the project link:

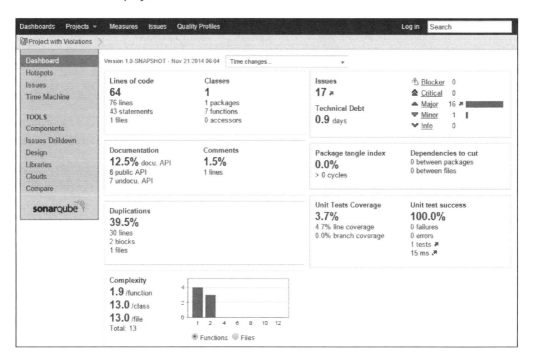

How it works...

The `sonar` goal of the Maven SonarQube plugin sets in motion a series of steps to do various analyses of the project. Based on the configuration, the Sonar plugin performs Checkstyle analysis, FindBugs analysis and PMD analysis, as well as detects code coverage, code duplication, design issues and code complexity.

It sends the output to a database and generates reports that can be viewed from the web page by the user.

As you can see from the dashboard, it has generated the unit test report along with coverage information. Clicking on the link will take the user to details of the coverage.

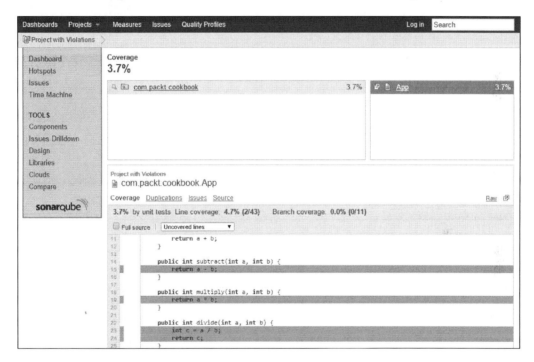

Similarly, clicking on **Issues** gives details of the various violations:

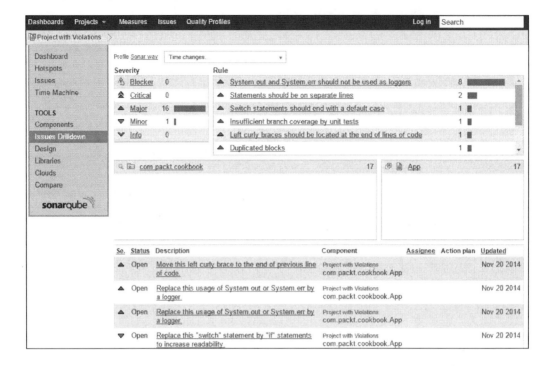

Each of these issues can be drilled down to the line-level details, and Sonar provides the details, including fix suggestions.

There's more...

SonarQube provides several configuration options to specify rules to be included/excluded, source files to be included/excluded, and so on. The configuration can be done through the web interface, and in some cases, by means of properties, either in the Maven's settings file or through the command line.

In addition, SonarQube provides plugins for Eclipse and IntelliJ. Once installed and configured, these plugins report violations directly in the IDE in the specific lines. As this is not specific to Maven, its details are outside the scope of this section.

7
Reporting and Documentation

In this chapter, we will see how we can use the Maven Site plugin, as well as configure various reports on a site. We will cover the following recipes:

- ▶ Documenting with the Maven Site plugin
- ▶ Generating Javadocs for a site
- ▶ Generating source cross-reference for a site
- ▶ Generating unit test reports for a site
- ▶ Generating code coverage reports for a site
- ▶ Generating code quality reports for a site
- ▶ Generating selective reports
- ▶ Deploying a site

Introduction

One of the most powerful features of Maven is the ability to create documentation for the project. It is useful to have a self-documenting project that can be published to a website without additional effort. Maven provides the ability to generate this documentation, known as a site report, and publish it to a website.

Many Maven plugins use the Site feature to generate project documentation. In fact, Maven itself uses the Site plugin to generate its website.

Documenting with the Maven Site plugin

Along with the `clean` and `default` lifecycle, Maven also consists of a `site` lifecycle. Like `clean`, `site` is implemented by a Maven plugin, in this case, the Maven Site plugin.

Getting ready

Maven is set up on your system and is verified for work. To do this, refer to the first three recipes of *Chapter 1, Getting Started*.

How to do it...

Use the following steps to generate documentation using the Maven Site plugin:

1. Open one of the Maven projects for which we need to generate a site report (for instance, `project-with-documentation`).

2. Run the following command:

   mvn site

3. Observe the output as shown in the following screenshot:

```
C:\projects\apache-maven-cookbook\simple-project>mvn site
[INFO] Scanning for projects...
[INFO]
[INFO] ------------------------------------------------------------------------
[INFO]
[INFO] Building simple-project 1.0-SNAPSHOT
[INFO]
[INFO]
[INFO] --- maven-site-plugin:3.3:site (default-site) @ simple-project ---
[WARNING] Report plugin org.apache.maven.plugins:maven-project-info-reports-plug
in has an empty version.
[WARNING]
[WARNING] It is highly recommended to fix these problems because they threaten t
he stability of your build.
[WARNING]
[WARNING] For this reason, future Maven versions might no longer support buildin
g such malformed projects.
[INFO] configuring report plugin org.apache.maven.plugins:maven-project-info-rep
orts-plugin:2.7
[INFO] Relativizing decoration links with respect to project URL: http://maven.a
pache.org
[INFO] Rendering site with org.apache.maven.skins:maven-default-skin:jar:1.0 ski
n.
[INFO] Generating "About" report         --- maven-project-info-reports-plugin:2.7
[INFO] Generating "Plugin Management" report       --- maven-project-info-reports-p
lugin:2.7
[INFO] Generating "Distribution Management" report     --- maven-project-info-rep
orts-plugin:2.7
[INFO] Generating "Dependency Information" report    --- maven-project-info-repo
rts-plugin:2.7
[INFO] Generating "Source Repository" report      --- maven-project-info-reports-p
lugin:2.7
[INFO] Generating "Mailing Lists" report        --- maven-project-info-reports-plugi
n:2.7
[INFO] Generating "Issue Tracking" report       --- maven-project-info-reports-plug
in:2.7
[INFO] Generating "Continuous Integration" report    --- maven-project-info-repo
rts-plugin:2.7
[INFO] Generating "Project Plugins" report       --- maven-project-info-reports-plu
gin:2.7
[INFO] Generating "Project License" report      --- maven-project-info-reports-plu
gin:2.7
[INFO] Generating "Project Team" report       --- maven-project-info-reports-plugin
:2.7
[INFO] Generating "Project Summary" report      --- maven-project-info-reports-plu
gin:2.7
[INFO] Generating "Dependencies" report       --- maven-project-info-reports-plugin
:2.7
[INFO] ------------------------------------------------------------------------
[INFO] BUILD SUCCESS
[INFO] ------------------------------------------------------------------------
```

4. Open the `index.html` file generated in the `target/site` folder:

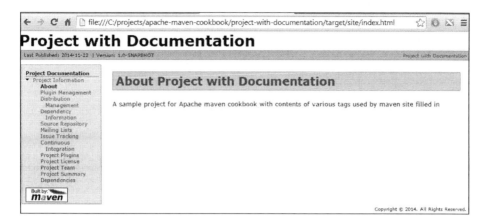

How it works...

`Site` is one of the Maven lifecycles. When the `mvn site` command is run, it invokes the `site` phase of the `site` lifecycle. The `site` goal of the Maven Site plugin is bound to this phase and is invoked.

The `site` goal performs a series of steps to generate the report. It uses various elements in the pom file related to this. Let us look at the various items in the default report:

Document	Description
About	A sample project for Apache maven cookbook with contents of various tags used by maven site filled in
Plugin Management	This document lists the plugins that are defined through pluginManagement.
Distribution Management	This document provides informations on the distribution management of this project.
Dependency Information	This document describes how to to include this project as a dependency using various dependency management tools.
Source Repository	This is a link to the online source repository that can be viewed via a web browser.
Mailing Lists	This document provides subscription and archive information for this project's mailing lists.
Issue Tracking	This is a link to the issue management system for this project. Issues (bugs, features, change requests) can be created and queried using this link.
Continuous Integration	This is a link to the definitions of all continuous integration processes that builds and tests code on a frequent, regular basis.
Project Plugins	This document lists the build plugins and the report plugins used by this project.
Project License	This is a link to the definitions of project licenses.
Project Team	This document provides information on the members of this project. These are the individuals who have contributed to the project in one form or another.
Project Summary	This document lists other related information of this project
Dependencies	This document lists the project's dependencies and provides information on each dependency.

In addition to this, the `site` command generates reports based on the contents of the `reporting` section of the pom:

```xml
<reporting>
  <plugins>
    <plugin>
      <artifactId>maven-project-info-reports-plugin</artifactId>
      <version>2.0.1</version>
      <reportSets>
        <reportSet></reportSet>
      </reportSets>
    </plugin>
  </plugins>
</reporting>
```

A number of Maven plugins can generate reports defined and configured under the `reporting` element. We will see many reports in the following sections.

There's more...

We have only seen what the default `site` command offers. The Maven Site plugin offers various configurations to make many more customizations. Some of them are as follows:

- Create a different documentation format: The default format of the site is APT (almost plain text), a wiki-like format

- Override the default navigation tree: This is required if you want to insert additional content in the site

- Creating skins: This is needed if you want to style the site reports differently

Let us see how to do some of these:

1. Add the `site.xml` file with the following content to the `src\site` folder of the `project-with-documentation` project folder:

```xml
<project xmlns="http://maven.apache.org/DECORATION/1.6.0"
xmlns:xsi="http://www.w3.org/2001/XMLSchema-instance"
xsi:schemaLocation="http://maven.apache.org/DECORATION/1.6.
0 http://maven.apache.org/xsd/decoration-1.6.0.xsd"
name="Project with Documentation">
    <bannerLeft>
        <name>Left Banner</name>
        <src>images/packt.png</src>
        <href>http://www.packtpub.com</href>
    </bannerLeft>
    <body>
```

```
        <menu name="Project with Documentation">
            <item name="Overview" href="index.html"/>
        </menu>
        <menu ref="reports"/>
    </body>
</project>
```

2. Add the image named `packt.png` to the `src\site\resources\images` folder.

3. Now, add the `index.apt` file in the `src\site\apt` folder with the following content:

    ```
    Welcome to Project with Documentation. This is a maven project
    created as part of apache maven cookbook by Packt Publishing.


    What is Project with Documentation?


    This maven project contains examples of how to use the site
    feature of maven.
    ```

4. Run the following command:

    mvn clean site

5. View the generated site report:

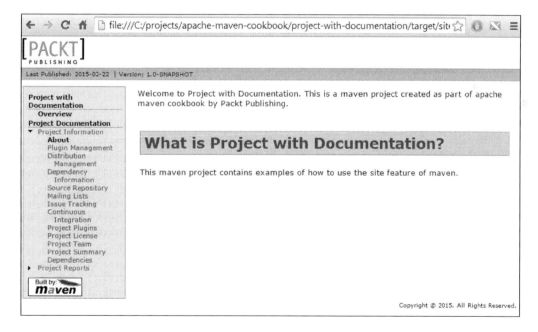

You can see a customized site page with the logo and the content that we specified.

Generating Javadocs for a site

Documentation for Java projects is created using Javadocs. Maven provides support not only to generate Javadocs, but also to publish them as part of the site. Plugins configured within the `reporting` element will generate content for the site. When they are configured within the `build` element, they can generate reports independent of site.

How to do it...

Use the following steps to generate Javadocs for a site:

1. Open the Maven project `project-with-documentation`.

2. Add the following section in the `pom.xml` file:

```xml
<reporting>
  <plugins>
    <plugin>
      <groupId>org.apache.maven.plugins</groupId>
      <artifactId>maven-javadoc-plugin</artifactId>
      <version>2.10.1</version>
    </plugin>
  </plugins>
</reporting>
```

3. Run the following command:

   mvn site

4. See the report generated:

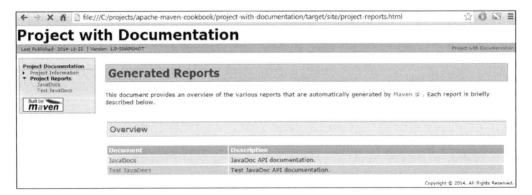

5. Click on the **JavaDocs** link:

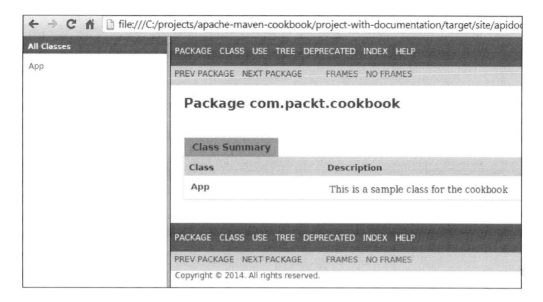

How it works...

We added the Javadoc plugin to the `reporting` section of `pom`. When the Site plugin runs, it examines this section and runs the reports configured there. In this case, it found `javadoc` and ran the relevant plugin to generate the Javadoc reports for the project.

Maven links the report from the site page in the **Project Reports** section.

There's more...

What if we do not want to document the test classes, but only the source? We can configure the plugin to do this by performing the following steps:

1. Add the following code to the `reporting` section where we set the value of `report` element to `javadoc`:

```
<reportSets>
  <reportSet>
    <reports>
      <report>javadoc</report>
    </reports>
  </reportSet>
</reportSets>
```

2. Run the following command:

```
mvn site
```

3. Open the resulting Site web page. Only the **JavaDocs** link is present on the site. The **Test JavaDocs** link is no longer present.

Generating source cross-reference for a site

In the previous chapter, we saw how the Maven JXR plugin generates source cross-reference. When publishing a project, it is useful to provide a way to refer to sources in addition to Javadocs. Let us see how to make that part of the site report.

How to do it...

Use the following steps to generate source cross-reference for a site:

1. Open the Maven project `project with documentation`.

2. Add the following code to the `reporting` section of the `pom.xml` file:

```
<plugin>
  <groupId>org.apache.maven.plugins</groupId>
  <artifactId>maven-jxr-plugin</artifactId>
  <version>2.5</version>
</plugin>
```

3. Run the following command:

```
mvn site
```

4. Open the generated site report:

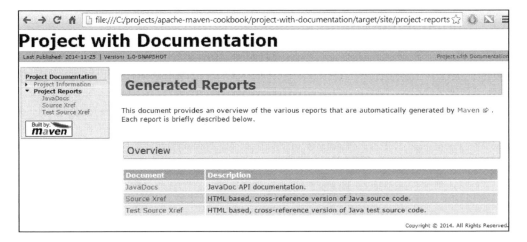

How it works...

Adding the Maven JXR plugin to the `reporting` section of pom automatically creates the project source cross-reference. By default, both source and test cross-references are generated. Like Javadoc, the `reportSet` element can be configured if we do not want a cross-reference for test classes.

Generating unit test reports for a site

When we have unit tests for our project, it will be good to see the test reports in the site documentation. Let us see how to do this.

How to do it...

Use the following steps to generate unit test reports for a site:

1. Open the Maven project for which you want to generate the site documentation (for instance, `project-with-documentation`).

2. Add the following code in the reporting section of the `pom.xml` file:

```
<plugin>
    <groupId>org.apache.maven.plugins</groupId>
    <artifactId>maven-surefire-report-plugin</artifactId>
    <version>2.18</version>
</plugin>
```

3. Run the following command:

```
mvn site
```

4. Observe the generated site report:

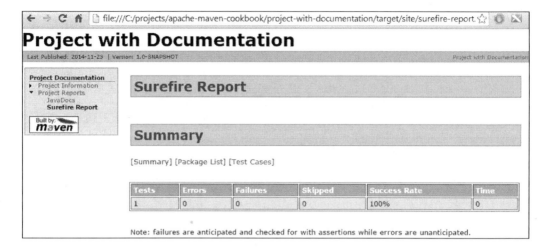

How it works...

If you recall, we use the Maven Surefire plugin to run tests. Surefire provides a Surefire Report plugin. When this plugin is added to the `reporting` section of the `pom.xml` file, it includes the test report in the site documentation.

The reports are identical, irrespective of whether JUnit or TestNG is used for unit testing.

In addition to the format of the report for the site, TestNG generates additional reports in a different format. These are available in the `target` folder but are not part of the site documentation.

Generating code coverage reports for a site

Let us now include code coverage from the unit tests of our project in the site documentation.

How to do it...

Use the following steps to generate code coverage reports for a site:

1. Open the Maven project for which you want to do this (for instance, `project-with-documentation`).

2. Add the following code in the `<build>` section of the `pom.xml` file:

```
<plugin>
    <groupId>org.jacoco</groupId>
```

```
    <artifactId>jacoco-maven-plugin</artifactId>
    <version>0.7.2.201409121644</version>
    <executions>
        <execution>
        <id>default-prepare-agent</id>
        <goals>
            <goal>prepare-agent</goal>
        </goals>
        </execution>
    </executions>
</plugin>
```

3. Add the following code in the `reporting` section of the `pom.xml` file:

```
<plugin>
    <groupId>org.jacoco</groupId>
    <artifactId>jacoco-maven-plugin</artifactId>
    <version>0.7.2.201409121644</version>
</plugin>
```

4. Run the following Maven command:

   mvn test site

5. Observe the site report as shown in following screenshot:

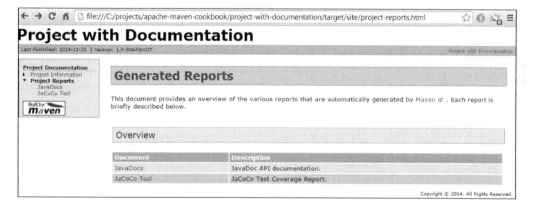

How it works...

The JaCoCo unit test coverage report shows up in site documentation on account of the following issues:

- As the `prepare-agent` goal of the JaCoCo plugin is added to the `build` section, Maven runs the JaCoCo agent

- As the `test` goal is run, Maven runs the test and the agent analyzes the tests for coverage

- As the JaCoCo plugin is added to the `reporting` section of the `pom.xml` file, the coverage report is generated and linked to the site documentation

- As you can see, the same plugin is added to the `build` and `reporting` section and does different things

There's more...

If you were to use Cobertura instead of JaCoCo to generate test coverage, you could do the following:

1. Remove the lines related to JaCoCo in the `build` and `reporting` sections.

2. Add the following code to the reporting section of the `pom.xml` file:

```
<plugin>
  <groupId>org.codehaus.mojo</groupId>
  <artifactId>cobertura-maven-plugin</artifactId>
  <version>2.6</version>
</plugin>
```

3. Run the following Maven command:

```
mvn site
```

4. Open the site documentation:

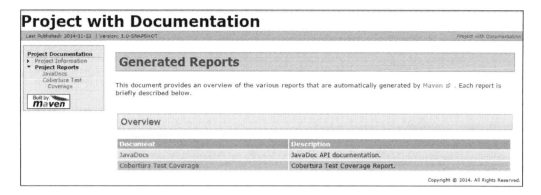

You will notice two things:

▶ We didn't need to specify anything in the `build` section

▶ We didn't need to run the `test` goal explicitly; the Maven Cobertura plugin did this.

Generating code quality reports for a site

We have seen how to use various code quality tools to perform static code analysis. Let us now see how we can update our site documentation with reports from these tools.

How to do it...

Use the following steps to generate code quality reports for a site:

1. Open the project for which we want to generate the site report.

2. Add the following code to the `reporting` section of the `pom.xml` file:

```
<plugin>
  <groupId>org.apache.maven.plugins</groupId>
  <artifactId>maven-pmd-plugin</artifactId>
  <version>3.3</version>
</plugin>
<plugin>
  <groupId>org.apache.maven.plugins</groupId>
  <artifactId>maven-checkstyle-plugin</artifactId>
  <version>2.13</version>
</plugin>
```

```
<plugin>
  <groupId>org.codehaus.mojo</groupId>
  <artifactId>findbugs-maven-plugin</artifactId>
  <version>3.0.0</version>
</plugin>>
```

3. Run the following Maven command:

   mvn test site

4. Open the generated site report:

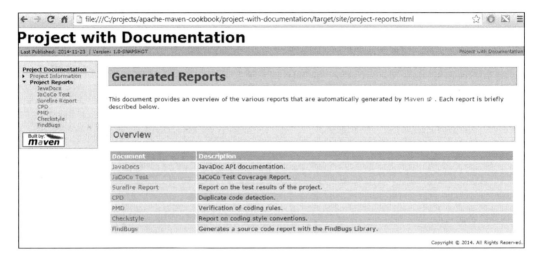

How it works...

For each of the code quality tools specified in the `reporting` section of the `pom.xml` file, the `site` goal runs the specified tool, generates the report, and links to the site documentation.

Clicking on each of the links takes the user to the specific report.

There's more...

If you have chosen to use SonarQube for analysis and want to link the Sonar report to the site documentation, then you can do the following:

1. Add the following code in the reporting section of the `pom.xml` file:

```
<plugin>
  <groupId>org.codehaus.sonar-plugins</groupId>
  <artifactId>maven-report</artifactId>
  <version>0.1</version>
</plugin>
```

2. Generate the site by running the following Maven command:

```
mvn test site
```

3. Open the site report:

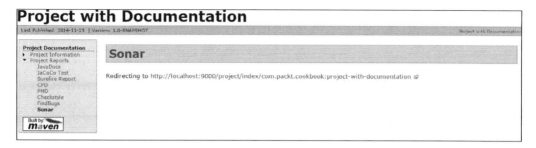

A new **Sonar** link is present in **Project Reports**, which automatically redirects to the default Sonar installation. The link can be customized to the appropriate URL, if it is different.

Generating selective reports

We have seen that by default the `site` command generates some **Project Information**. Some of it, for instance **Mailing Lists**, may be nonexistent or irrelevant to the project. Let us see how we can avoid generating these. The Maven Project Info Reports plugin is the plugin that provides the standard reports from pom. It can be configured to exclude specific reports.

How to do it...

Use the following steps to generate selective site report:

1. Open the project for which you want to generate the site report.

2. Add the following code to the `reporting` section of the `pom.xml` file:

```
<plugin>
    <groupId>org.apache.maven.plugins</groupId>
    <artifactId>maven-project-info-reports-plugin</artifactId>
    <version>2.7</version>
    <reportSets>
      <reportSet>
        <reports>
          <report>dependencies</report>
          <report>project-team</report>
          <report>license</report>
          <report>scm</report>
```

```
            </reports>
          </reportSet>
        </reportSets>
      </plugin>
```

3. Run the following Maven `site` command:

    mvn test site

4. Open the generated report:

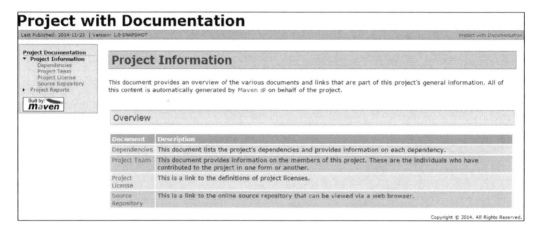

How it works...

We explicitly specified the reports that we wanted to see in **Project Information**. Due to this, only those reports are generated and displayed.

This allows us to avoid generating and displaying reports that are not applicable to the project.

Deploying a site

Once a site report is generated, it needs to be published. While this can be done manually, Maven also provides facilities to do this. Let us see how.

Getting ready

To publish a site, you need to have access to the web server where the site has to be deployed.

How to do it...

To deploy a site, use the following steps:

1. Add the following code to your `pom.xml` file. This could also be added in `settings.xml`:

```
<distributionManagement>
  <site>
    <id>myorg</id>
    <url>scp://www.myorg.com/project/</url>
  </site>
</distributionManagement>
```

2. For the corresponding ID, add the relevant username and password in your `settings.xml` file:

```
<servers>
  <server>
    <id>myorg</id>
    <username>username</username>
    <password>password</password>
    <filePermissions>664</filePermissions>
    <directoryPermissions>775</directoryPermissions>
  </server>
</servers>
```

3. Run the following Maven command:

```
mvn site-deploy
```

How it works...

When the `site-deploy` goal is run, Maven first builds the site. Then, it uses the entry set in the `distributionManagement` element to determine how the site needs to be deployed. The first part of the URL is the protocol to be used to transfer the file. In this case, it is `scp`. It uses the credentials specified in the `settings.xml` file and transfers the file to the destination.

There's more...

If you want to test your site before deploying, you can easily do so in the following way:

1. Run the following Maven command:

```
mvn site:run
```

2. Open the browser and go to `http://localhost:8080`:

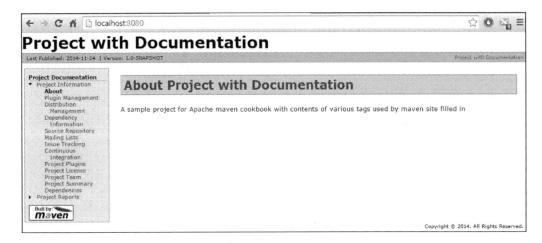

The run goal of the Maven Site plugin deploys the site in a **jetty server**, which is started by default by port `8080`. This allows you to view the site report and verify it before publishing.

8

Handling Typical Build Requirements

In this chapter, we will cover the following recipes:

- ▶ Including and excluding additional resources
- ▶ Including and excluding source files and folders
- ▶ Configuring Maven to search for plugins
- ▶ Working in offline mode
- ▶ Controlling the verbosity of the Maven output
- ▶ Using the Maven Help plugin
- ▶ Using the Maven SCM plugin
- ▶ Generating changelogs for a site

Introduction

In previous chapters, we have seen how to set up Apache Maven to build software projects. We have also seen how to configure it to analyze code quality and code coverage. We have seen how to generate and publish project documentation.

As we use Apache Maven, we will encounter requirements that are not generic, but at the same time, not rare. In many projects, there would be a need to include additional source or resource folders. We will see how Maven allows us to do this. We would also want to get more verbose output from Maven to help troubleshoot when things go wrong. We will also see to what extent we can get the Maven build working without the Internet. We will also see how Maven works with **software configuration management** (**SCM**) systems and allows SCM changes to be part of project documentation.

Including and excluding additional resources

There are many situations where you will need to include additional resource files or folders for compilation or testing. You might also have to exclude specific files or folders. Let us see how we can do this.

Getting ready

Maven is set up on your system and is verified for work. To do this, refer to the first three recipes of *Chapter 1, Getting Started*.

How to do it...

1. Open one of the Maven projects for which we need to include or exclude files or folders; for instance, `project-with-include-exclude`.

2. Add the following to the `build` section of your `pom` file:

```
<resources>
        <resource>
          <directory>src/resources/xml</directory>
          <includes>
             <include>*.xml</include>
          </includes>
        </resource>
        <resource>
          <directory>src/resources/json</directory>
          <includes>
             <include>include.json</include>
          </includes>
          <excludes>
             <exclude>exclude.json</exclude>
          </excludes>
        </resource>
</resources>
```

3. Run the following command:

```
mvn resources:resources
```

4. Observe the output:

```
[INFO] --- maven-resources-plugin:2.6:resources (default-cli) @
project-with-include-exclude ---
[INFO] Using 'UTF-8' encoding to copy filtered resources.
[INFO] Copying 2 resources
[INFO] Copying 1 resource
[INFO] ------------------------------------------------------------
-------------
```

5. View the contents of the `resources` folder:

6. View the contents of the build output directory:

How it works...

The `resources` goal of the Maven Resources plugin copies all the resources required by the source to build the output directory. This goal is bound to the `process-resources` phase, which is part of the `default` lifecycle.

By default, the goal copies over the contents of `src/main/resources`. When the `resources` tag is specified in the `pom` file, it copies the contents of the directories specified there, based on the `include` and `exclude` filters specified.

In our specific example, we did three things:

- ▶ Included all the XML files in the `src/resources/xml` folder
- ▶ Included a specific file in the `src/resources/json` folder
- ▶ Excluded a specific file in the `src/resouces/json` folder

There's more...

What if we need to copy test resources selectively? For this, we would need to do the following:

1. Add the following in the `build` section of your `pom` file:

```
<testResources>
  <testResource>
    <directory>src/resources/xml</directory>
    <includes>
      <include>*.xml</include>
    </includes>
  </testResource>
  <testResource>
    <directory>src/resources/json</directory>
    <includes>
      <include>include.json</include>
    </includes>
    <excludes>
      <exclude>exclude.json</exclude>
    </excludes>
  </testResource>
</testResources>
```

2. Run the following command:

```
mvn resources:testResources
```

3. View the contents of the `test-classes` folder:

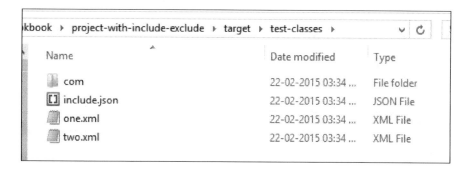

This will now copy over the specified test resources to the test output directory (`target/test-classes`).

We saw that the `resources` and `testResources` goals copied resources to `classes` and `test-classes` respectively. What if we need to copy these to specific folders, For instance, `xml` files to the `xml` folder and `json` files to the `json` folder? The `add-resource` and `add-test-resource` goals of the Build Helper Maven plugin come to our assistance here.

1. Update the `pom` file with the following code:

```
<plugin>
  <groupId>org.codehaus.mojo</groupId>
  <artifactId>build-helper-maven-plugin</artifactId>
  <version>1.9.1</version>
  <executions>
    <execution>
      <id>add-resource</id>
      <phase>generate-resources</phase>
      <goals>
        <goal>add-resource</goal>
      </goals>
      <configuration>
        <resources>
          <resource>
            <directory>src/resources/xml</directory>
            <targetPath>xml</targetPath>
          </resource>
          <resource>
            <directory>src/resources/json</directory>
            <targetPath>json</targetPath>
              <includes>
```

```
            <include>include.json</include>
         </includes>
         <excludes>
            <exclude>exclude.json</exclude>
         </excludes>
       </resource>
      </resources>
     </configuration>
   </execution>
  </executions>
</plugin>
```

2. Run the following command:

   mvn compile

3. Examine the `target/classes` folder now.

You will see the `xml` and `json` subfolders with their respective content.

Including and excluding source files and folders

As per Maven conventions, all project sources should be in the `src` folder. However, there may be legacy projects that are organized differently and may have more than one source folder. Also, in some projects, we might generate sources dynamically from tools such as `wsdl2java`. In such cases, Maven needs to be told about these additional source folders. Note that such projects may not work well in IDEs.

How to do it...

Use the following steps to include and exclude source files and folders in your Maven project:

1. Open the Maven project named `project-with-additional-source`.

2. Add the following section in the `pom` file:

```
<plugin>
    <groupId>org.codehaus.mojo</groupId>
    <artifactId>build-helper-maven-plugin</artifactId>
    <version>1.9.1</version>
    <executions>
      <execution>
        <id>add-source</id>
        <phase>generate-sources</phase>
        <goals>
           <goal>add-source</goal>
        </goals>
```

```
<configuration>
  <sources>
    <source>src/main/source</source>
  </sources>
</configuration>
</execution>
</executions>
</plugin>
```

3. Run the following command:

    mvn compile

4. See the output generated:

    [INFO] --- build-helper-maven-plugin:1.9.1:add-source (add-source) @ project-with-additional-source ---

    [INFO] Source directory: C:\projects\apache-maven-cookbook\ project-with-additional-source\src\main\source added.

5. View the `target/classes` folder:

```
Directory of C:\projects\apache-maven-cookbook\project-with-additional-source\t
arget\classes\com\packt\cookbook

30-11-2014  14:59    <DIR>          .
30-11-2014  14:59    <DIR>          ..
30-11-2014  14:59               390 AdditionalSource.class
30-11-2014  14:59               551 App.class
               2 File(s)            941 bytes
```

How it works...

We had an additional source folder called `src/main/source`. We specified this in the `configuration` section of the Build Helper Maven plugin. We also bound the `add-source` goal of the plugin to the `generate-sources` phase of the `default` lifecycle.

As part of the `default` lifecycle, the `generate-sources` phase is run by Maven prior to the `compile` goal. This invokes the `add-source` goal of the plugin, which adds the additional folder and its contents for compilation.

In a similar way, additional test folders can be added to the build. The configuration would be identical to the earlier case, except for the `execution` section, which would be as follows:

```
<execution>
  <id>add-test-source</id>
  <phase>generate-test-sources</phase>
  <goals>
    <goal>add-test-source</goal>
```

```
        </goals>
        <configuration>
          <sources>
            <source>src/main/source</source>
          </sources>
        </configuration>
      </execution>
```

We specify the `add-test-source` goal instead of `add-source` and bind it to the `generate-test-sources` phase.

There's more...

The Build Helper Maven plugin provides a number of other goals that meet specific project requirements. Here are some of them:

▶ `attach-artifact`: This is used to attach additional artifacts to be installed and/or deployed, besides the project artifact. This would be done by configuring the plugin as follows:

```
<plugin>
  <groupId>org.codehaus.mojo</groupId>
  <artifactId>build-helper-maven-plugin</artifactId>
  <version>1.9.1</version>
  <executions>
    <execution>
      <id>attach-artifacts</id>
      <phase>package</phase>
      <goals>
        <goal>attach-artifact</goal>
      </goals>
      <configuration>
        <artifacts>
          <artifact>
            <file>some file</file>
            <type>extension of your file </type>
            <classifier>optional</classifier>
          </artifact>
        </artifacts>
      </configuration>
    </execution>
  </executions>
</plugin>
```

▶ `maven-version`: This is used to set a property containing the current version of Maven, which can be used as required. To use the Maven version number in the manifest of the project JAR, we will configure the plugin as follows:

```
<build>
  <plugins>
    <plugin>
      <groupId>org.codehaus.mojo</groupId>
      <artifactId>build-helper-maven-plugin</artifactId>
      <version>1.9.1</version>
      <executions>
        <execution>
          <id>maven-version</id>
          <goals>
            <goal>maven-version</goal>
          </goals>
        </execution>
      </executions>
    </plugin>
    <plugin>
      <groupId>org.apache.maven.plugins</groupId>
      <artifactId>maven-jar-plugin</artifactId>
      <version>2.2</version>
      <configuration>
        <archive>
          <manifestEntries>
            <Maven-Version>${maven.version}</Maven-Version>
          </manifestEntries>
        </archive>
      </configuration>
    </plugin>
  </plugins>
</build>
```

Configuring Maven to search for plugins

You will recall that in the section on using the Maven JaCoCo plugin, to generate code coverage we had to explicitly specify the `projectId` and `artifactId` values of the plugin to it from the command line. However, for most other plugins, we specified the plugin name without additional information.

We will see why we had to do this and how to avoid it.

How to do it...

1. Open the `settings` file (specifically the `settings.xml` file in your home directory).

2. Add the following section:

```
<pluginGroups>
    <pluginGroup>org.jacoco</pluginGroup>
</pluginGroups>
```

3. Run the following command on the same project for which you ran JaCoCo earlier:

`mvn clean jacoco:prepare-agent test jacoco:report`

4. Observe the output:

```
[INFO]
[INFO] --- jacoco-maven-plugin:0.7.2.201409121644:report (default-
cli) @ project-with-tests ---
[INFO] Analyzed bundle 'Project with Tests' with 1 classes
```

How it works...

There are two types of Maven plugins, which are as follows:

- Plugins maintained by the Maven team itself (let us call them official plugins). These are in the default plugin groups `org.apache.maven.plugins` and `org.codehaus.mojo`.

- All other plugins (let's say third-party plugins).

All official plugins have the same `groupId`, namely `org.apache.maven.plugins`. They also have a convention for `artifactId`: `maven-${prefix}-plugin`, where `prefix` stands for the plugin prefix, the short name to refer to the plugin.

The prefix used to reference the plugin can be customized as well. The prefix can be specified directly through the `goalPrefix` configuration parameter on the `Maven-plugin-plugin` of the plugin's `pom` file.

So, when we run `mvn clean`, Maven looks for the `maven-clean-plugin` in the `org.apache.maven.plugins` group.

What about third-party plugins? `pluginGroups` lets Maven know the `groupId` where it should search for additional plugins. So in the earlier case, Maven searched for plugins in the `org.jacoco` group.

Third-party plugins should be named differently from official plugins. The conventional way to define the `artifactId` for third-party plugins is `${prefix}-maven-plugin`. When specified in this way, Maven automatically identifies the shortcut name for the plugin. In the earlier case, as the `artifactId` is `jacoco-maven-plugin`, the shortcut is `jacoco`.

There's more...

Maven will always search specified `pluginGroups` before it searches the following default groups:

- `org.apache.maven.plugins`
- `org.codehaus.mojo`

Maven takes the first match for the shortcut that it finds. For instance, if there is a `clean` shortcut in a user-specified plugin in `pluginGroups`, it will take precedence over a Maven Clean plugin.

Working in offline mode

There might be situations where a Maven project needs to be built without access to the Internet. Let us see how Maven supports this, as well as the caveats.

How to do it...

1. Open a project that you want to build offline.
2. Run the following command:

```
mvn dependency:go-offline
```

3. Observe the output:

```
C:\projects\apache-maven-cookbook\simple-project>mvn dependency:go-offline
[INFO] Scanning for projects...
[INFO]
[INFO] ------------------------------------------------------------------------
[INFO] Building simple-project 1.0-SNAPSHOT
[INFO] ------------------------------------------------------------------------
[INFO] >>> maven-dependency-plugin:2.8:go-offline (default-cli) > :resolve-plugi
ns @ simple-project >>>
[INFO]
[INFO] --- maven-dependency-plugin:2.8:resolve-plugins (resolve-plugins) @ simpl
e-project ---
[INFO] Plugin Resolved: maven-install-plugin-2.4.jar
[INFO]       Plugin Dependency Resolved: maven-plugin-api-2.0.6.jar
[INFO]       Plugin Dependency Resolved: maven-project-2.0.6.jar
[INFO]       Plugin Dependency Resolved: maven-model-2.0.6.jar
[INFO]       Plugin Dependency Resolved: maven-artifact-manager-2.0.6.jar
[INFO]       Plugin Dependency Resolved: maven-artifact-2.0.6.jar
[INFO]       Plugin Dependency Resolved: plexus-utils-3.0.5.jar
[INFO]       Plugin Dependency Resolved: plexus-digest-1.0.jar
[INFO] Plugin Resolved: maven-clean-plugin-2.5.jar
[INFO]       Plugin Dependency Resolved: maven-plugin-api-2.0.6.jar
[INFO]       Plugin Dependency Resolved: plexus-utils-3.0.jar
[INFO] Plugin Resolved: maven-compiler-plugin-3.1.jar
[INFO]       Plugin Dependency Resolved: maven-plugin-api-2.0.9.jar
[INFO]       Plugin Dependency Resolved: maven-artifact-2.0.9.jar
[INFO]       Plugin Dependency Resolved: maven-core-2.0.9.jar
[INFO]       Plugin Dependency Resolved: maven-toolchain-1.0.jar
[INFO]       Plugin Dependency Resolved: maven-shared-utils-0.1.jar
[INFO]       Plugin Dependency Resolved: maven-shared-incremental-1.1.jar
[INFO]       Plugin Dependency Resolved: plexus-compiler-api-2.2.jar
[INFO]       Plugin Dependency Resolved: plexus-compiler-manager-2.2.jar
[INFO]       Plugin Dependency Resolved: plexus-compiler-javac-2.2.jar
[INFO]       Plugin Dependency Resolved: plexus-container-default-1.5.5.jar
[INFO] Plugin Resolved: maven-jar-plugin-2.4.jar
[INFO]       Plugin Dependency Resolved: maven-plugin-api-2.0.6.jar
[INFO]       Plugin Dependency Resolved: maven-project-2.0.6.jar
[INFO]       Plugin Dependency Resolved: maven-model-2.0.6.jar
[INFO]       Plugin Dependency Resolved: maven-artifact-2.0.6.jar
[INFO]       Plugin Dependency Resolved: maven-archiver-2.5.jar
[INFO]       Plugin Dependency Resolved: plexus-archiver-2.1.jar
[INFO]       Plugin Dependency Resolved: commons-lang-2.1.jar
[INFO]       Plugin Dependency Resolved: plexus-utils-3.0.jar
[INFO] Plugin Resolved: maven-site-plugin-3.3.jar
[INFO]       Plugin Dependency Resolved: maven-reporting-exec-1.1.jar
[INFO]       Plugin Dependency Resolved: maven-core-3.0.jar
[INFO]       Plugin Dependency Resolved: maven-model-3.0.jar
[INFO]       Plugin Dependency Resolved: maven-plugin-api-3.0.jar
[INFO]       Plugin Dependency Resolved: maven-settings-3.0.jar
[INFO]       Plugin Dependency Resolved: maven-settings-builder-3.0.jar
[INFO]       Plugin Dependency Resolved: maven-archiver-2.4.2.jar
[INFO]       Plugin Dependency Resolved: doxia-sink-api-1.4.jar
[INFO]       Plugin Dependency Resolved: doxia-logging-api-1.4.jar
[INFO]       Plugin Dependency Resolved: doxia-core-1.4.jar
[INFO]       Plugin Dependency Resolved: doxia-module-xhtml-1.4.jar
[INFO]       Plugin Dependency Resolved: doxia-module-apt-1.4.jar
[INFO]       Plugin Dependency Resolved: doxia-module-xdoc-1.4.jar
[INFO]       Plugin Dependency Resolved: doxia-module-fml-1.4.jar
[INFO]       Plugin Dependency Resolved: doxia-module-markdown-1.4.jar
[INFO]       Plugin Dependency Resolved: servlet-api-2.5.jar
[INFO]
```

4. Run the following command:

```
mvn -o clean package
```

Observe that the build is completed successfully without any network connection.

How it works...

The `go-offline` goal of the Maven Dependency plugin downloads all the required dependencies and plugins for the project, based on the pom file. The `-o` option tells Maven to work offline and not check the Internet for anything.

However, it is not without its issues. On a brand new local repository, the `offline` option will not work with the following error:

```
[INFO] ----------------------------------------------------------------------
[ERROR] Failed to execute goal org.apache.maven.plugins:maven-resources-plugin:2
.6:resources (default-resources) on project simple-project: Execution default-re
sources of goal org.apache.maven.plugins:maven-resources-plugin:2.6:resources fa
iled: A required class was missing while executing org.apache.maven.plugins:mave
n-resources-plugin:2.6:resources: Lorg/sonatype/plexus/build/incremental/BuildCo
ntext;
[ERROR] ----------------------------------------------------------------------
[ERROR] realm =      plugin>org.apache.maven.plugins:maven-resources-plugin:2.6
[ERROR] strategy = org.codehaus.plexus.classworlds.strategy.SelfFirstStrategy
[ERROR] urls[0] = file:/C:/Users/raghu/.m2/repository/org/apache/maven/plugins/m
aven-resources-plugin/2.6/maven-resources-plugin-2.6.jar
```

This is a known problem or limitation with the Maven Dependency plugin. The required project has to be built online once to download anything that is missed out by the plugin. Subsequently, the project can be built offline. This is typically not required, as most organizations use a repository manager, such as Nexus or Artifactory, if they do not allow direct Internet access.

 If your project uses SNAPSHOT dependencies, then Maven will need the Internet to look for updates to the dependencies. To avoid this, you can set the `updatePolicy` to `never`, but this would be counterproductive as you will not get the latest version of the dependency.

There's more...

Another way to run Maven in offline mode is to specify the `offline` parameter as `true` in the `settings` file. Once this is done, no attempt is made by Maven to connect to the Internet.

1. Add the following in the settings file:

   ```
   <offline>true</offline>
   ```

2. Run a Maven build:

   mvn clean package

Observe that the build is completed successfully without connecting to the Internet.

Controlling the verbosity of the Maven output

Sometimes, the output from Maven might be too verbose and we may want to only see the errors. At other times, the information displayed by Maven may be insufficient and we want to see more details. Let us see how we can control this.

How to do it...

1. Open a Maven project.

2. Run the following command:

    ```
    mvn -q clean package
    ```

3. Observe the output:

    ```
    C:\projects\apache-maven-cookbook\simple-project>mvn -q clean package
    -----------------------------------------------------------------------
     T E S T S
    -----------------------------------------------------------------------
    Running com.packt.cookbook.AppTest
    Tests run: 1, Failures: 0, Errors: 0, Skipped: 0, Time elapsed: 0.01 sec

    Results :

    Tests run: 1, Failures: 0, Errors: 0, Skipped: 0

    C:\projects\apache-maven-cookbook\simple-project>
    ```

4. Now run the following command:

    ```
    mvn -X clean package
    ```

5. Observe the output:

```
[DEBUG]    Excluded: org.apache.maven:maven-project:jar:2.0.6
[DEBUG]    Excluded: org.apache.maven:maven-settings:jar:2.0.6
[DEBUG]    Excluded: org.apache.maven:maven-profile:jar:2.0.6
[DEBUG]    Excluded: org.apache.maven:maven-artifact-manager:jar:2.0.6
[DEBUG]    Excluded: org.apache.maven:maven-repository-metadata:jar:2.0.6
[DEBUG]    Excluded: org.apache.maven:maven-plugin-registry:jar:2.0.6
[DEBUG]    Excluded: org.codehaus.plexus:plexus-container-default:jar:1.0-alpha-9
-stable-1
[DEBUG]    Excluded: classworlds:classworlds:jar:1.1-alpha-2
[DEBUG]    Excluded: org.apache.maven:maven-model:jar:2.0.6
[DEBUG]    Excluded: org.apache.maven:maven-artifact:jar:2.0.6
[DEBUG]    Excluded: org.apache.maven:maven-core:jar:2.0.6
[DEBUG]    Excluded: org.apache.maven:maven-plugin-parameter-documenter:jar:2.0.6

[DEBUG]    Excluded: org.apache.maven:maven-error-diagnostics:jar:2.0.6
[DEBUG]    Excluded: org.apache.maven:maven-plugin-descriptor:jar:2.0.6
[DEBUG]    Excluded: org.apache.maven:maven-monitor:jar:2.0.6
[DEBUG] Configuring mojo org.apache.maven.plugins:maven-jar-plugin:2.4:jar from
plugin realm ClassRealm[plugin>org.apache.maven.plugins:maven-jar-plugin:2.4, pa
rent: sun.misc.Launcher$AppClassLoader@33d626a4]
[DEBUG] Configuring mojo 'org.apache.maven.plugins:maven-jar-plugin:2.4:jar' wit
h basic configurator -->
[DEBUG]    (f) classesDirectory = C:\projects\apache-maven-cookbook\simple-projec
t\target\classes
[DEBUG]    (f) defaultManifestFile = C:\projects\apache-maven-cookbook\simple-pro
ject\target\classes\META-INF\MANIFEST.MF
[DEBUG]    (f) finalName = simple-project-1.0-SNAPSHOT
[DEBUG]    (f) forceCreation = false
[DEBUG]    (f) outputDirectory = C:\projects\apache-maven-cookbook\simple-project
\target
[DEBUG]    (f) project = MavenProject: com.packt.cookbook:simple-project:1.0-SNAP
SHOT @ C:\projects\apache-maven-cookbook\simple-project\pom.xml
[DEBUG]    (f) session = org.apache.maven.execution.MavenSession@2a3a0cee
[DEBUG]    (f) skipIfEmpty = false
[DEBUG]    (f) useDefaultManifestFile = false
[DEBUG] -- end configuration --
[DEBUG] isUp2date: false (Destination C:\projects\apache-maven-cookbook\simple-p
roject\target\simple-project-1.0-SNAPSHOT.jar not found.)
[INFO] Building jar: C:\projects\apache-maven-cookbook\simple-project\target\sim
ple-project-1.0-SNAPSHOT.jar
[DEBUG] adding directory META-INF/
[DEBUG] adding entry META-INF/MANIFEST.MF
[DEBUG] adding directory com/
[DEBUG] adding directory com/packt/
[DEBUG] adding directory com/packt/cookbook/
[DEBUG] adding entry com/packt/cookbook/App.class
[DEBUG] adding directory META-INF/maven/
[DEBUG] adding directory META-INF/maven/com.packt.cookbook/
[DEBUG] adding directory META-INF/maven/com.packt.cookbook/simple-project/
[DEBUG] adding entry META-INF/maven/com.packt.cookbook/simple-project/pom.xml
[DEBUG] adding entry META-INF/maven/com.packt.cookbook/simple-project/pom.proper
ties
[INFO] ------------------------------------------------------------------------
[INFO] BUILD SUCCESS
[INFO] ------------------------------------------------------------------------
[INFO] Total time: 3.656 s
[INFO] Finished at: 2014-11-30T17:09:34+05:30
[INFO] Final Memory: 13M/159M
[INFO] ------------------------------------------------------------------------
C:\projects\apache-maven-cookbook\simple-project>
```

How it works...

Maven provides different levels of logging. The typical levels are DEBUG (detailed messages), INFO (information messages), and ERROR (error messages). Specifying a level displays all messages at and above that level. For instance, specifying the INFO level displays messages at the INFO and ERROR levels.

By default, Maven logs all INFO level messages to the screen.

The -q parameter tells Maven to be quiet and not display anything other than ERROR level messages on the screen. So the only display is the output from tests.

On the other hand, the -X parameter tells Maven to display all messages at the DEBUG level and above. This gives a lot of information, which is useful for troubleshooting issues.

There's more...

Instead of viewing the Maven output on the screen, you could redirect it to a file to be viewed later. To do this, run the following command:

```
mvn -l simple-project-log.txt clean package
```

The command will be completed with no output on the screen. The `simple-project-log.txt` file will contain all the log messages. You can use a combination of `-l` along with `-q` or `-X` to redirect the appropriate level of logging to the file.

Alternately, the output can be redirected to a file:

```
mvn clean package > simple-project-log.txt
```

Using the Maven Help plugin

Maven provides a `-h` command-line flag to display various command-line parameters that it supports. However, there is a Help plugin that helps you get other information.

How to do it...

1. Open the simple Maven project.

2. Run the following command:

   ```
   mvn help:effective-pom
   ```

3. Observe the output:

```
C:\projects\apache-maven-cookbook\simple-project>mvn help:effective-pom
[INFO] Scanning for projects...
[INFO]
[INFO] ------------------------------------------------------------------------
[INFO] Building simple-project 1.0-SNAPSHOT
[INFO] ------------------------------------------------------------------------
[INFO]
[INFO]
[INFO] --- maven-help-plugin:2.2:effective-pom (default-cli) @ simple-project ---
[INFO]
Effective POMs, after inheritance, interpolation, and profiles are applied:

<!-- ====================================================================== -->
<!--                                                                        -->
<!-- Generated by Maven Help Plugin on 2014-11-30T05:31:17                  -->
<!-- See: http://maven.apache.org/plugins/maven-help-plugin/                -->
<!--                                                                        -->
<!-- ====================================================================== -->

<!-- ====================================================================== -->
<!--                                                                        -->
<!-- Effective POM for project                                              -->
<!-- 'com.packt.cookbook:simple-project:jar:1.0-SNAPSHOT'                   -->
<!--                                                                        -->
<!-- ====================================================================== -->

<project xmlns="http://maven.apache.org/POM/4.0.0" xmlns:xsi="http://www.w3.org/
2001/XMLSchema-instance" xsi:schemaLocation="http://maven.apache.org/POM/4.0.0 h
ttp://maven.apache.org/xsd/maven-4.0.0.xsd">
  <modelVersion>4.0.0</modelVersion>
  <groupId>com.packt.cookbook</groupId>
  <artifactId>simple-project</artifactId>
  <version>1.0-SNAPSHOT</version>
  <name>simple-project</name>
```

4. Run the following command on a project with a profile (for instance, `project-with-profile`):

```
mvn help:all-profiles
```

5. Observe the output:

```
[INFO] --- maven-help-plugin:2.2:all-profiles (default-cli) @
project-with-profile ---
```

```
[INFO] Listing Profiles for Project: com.packt.cookbook:project-
with-profile:jar
```

```
:1.0-SNAPSHOT
```

```
  Profile Id: dev (Active: false , Source: pom)
```

6. Run the following command:

```
mvn -help:active-profiles
```

7. Observe the output:

```
Active Profiles for Project 'com.packt.cookbook:project-with-
profile:jar:1.0-SNAPSHOT':
```

```
The following profiles are active:
```

8. Now run the following command:

```
mvn -Pdev help:active-profiles
```

9. Observe the output:

```
Active Profiles for Project 'com.packt.cookbook:project-with-
profile:jar:1.0-SNAPSHOT':
```

```
The following profiles are active:
```

```
  - dev (source: com.packt.cookbook:project-with-profile:1.0-
SNAPSHOT)
```

How it works...

The Maven Help plugin provides different goals. These are also supported by IDEs, and are as follows:

▶ `effective-pom`: This displays the pom file that will be used by Maven after applying inheritance, interpolation, and profiles. This is useful to know the final pom file when it is needed for troubleshooting.

- ▶ all-profiles: This goal displays all the profiles that are available for the project. It indicates whether the profiles are active or not.

- ▶ active-profiles: This goal displays the list of active profiles. We explicitly enabled the dev profile (which was not active by default), so it showed up in the list of active profiles.

There's more...

The Maven Help plugin provides a few other goals as well. A notable one is the describe goal, which is used to get details of any plugin.

1. To understand this, let's use an instance and run the following command:

   ```
   mvn help:describe -DgroupId=org.jacoco
   -DartifactId=jacoco-maven-plugin -Ddetail=true
   ```

2. Observe the results:

```
[INFO] --- maven-help-plugin:2.2:describe (default-cli) @ standalone-pom ---
[INFO] org.jacoco:jacoco-maven-plugin:0.7.2.201409121644

Name: JaCoCo :: Maven Plugin
Description: The JaCoCo Maven Plugin provides the JaCoCo runtime agent to
  your tests and allows basic report creation.
Group Id: org.jacoco
Artifact Id: jacoco-maven-plugin
Version: 0.7.2.201409121644
Goal Prefix: jacoco

This plugin has 10 goals:

jacoco:check
  Description: Checks that the code coverage metrics are being met.
  Implementation: org.jacoco.maven.CheckMojo
  Language: java
  Bound to phase: verify

  Available parameters:
```

 The describe goal does not need you to have a Maven project. You are just getting some help information for a particular plugin!

Using the Maven SCM plugin

Maven provides a mechanism to interact with SCM systems in a vendor-independent way. Typically, a Maven project is checked in an SCM. Using the Maven SCM plugin, you can perform a number of SCM-related activities.

Getting ready

The Maven project that we want to use the plugin with should be in an SCM. Maven supports a number of SCM providers. We will use Git to illustrate this.

How to do it...

1. Add the following code to your pom file:

```
<scm>
        <connection>scm:git:https://bitbucket.org/maruhgar/apache-maven-cookbook</connection>
    <developerConnection>scm:git:https://maruhgar@bitbucket.org/maruhgar/apache-maven-cookbook</developerConnection>
        <url>https://bitbucket.org/maruhgar/apache-maven-cookbook</url>
    </scm>
```

2. Run the following command:

```
mvn scm:status
```

3. Observe the output in Windows:

```
[INFO] --- maven-scm-plugin:1.9.2:status (default-cli) @ project-with-documentat
ion ---
[INFO] Executing: cmd.exe /X /C "git rev-parse --show-toplevel"
[INFO] Working directory: C:\projects\apache-maven-cookbook\project-with-documen
tation
[INFO] Executing: cmd.exe /X /C "git status --porcelain ."
[INFO] Working directory: C:\projects\apache-maven-cookbook\project-with-documen
tation
[INFO] modified status for project-with-documentation/pom.xml
```

4. For Linux, the output will be as follows:

```
[INFO] --- maven-scm-plugin:1.9.2:status (default-cli) @ project-with-documentat
ion ---
[INFO] Executing: /bin/sh -c cd /home/raghu/projects/apache-maven-cookbook/proje
ct-with-documentation && git rev-parse --show-toplevel
[INFO] Working directory: /home/raghu/projects/apache-maven-cookbook/project-wit
h-documentation
[INFO] Executing: /bin/sh -c cd /home/raghu/projects/apache-maven-cookbook/proje
ct-with-documentation && git status --porcelain .
[INFO] Working directory: /home/raghu/projects/apache-maven-cookbook/project-wit
h-documentation
```

How it works...

When the `status` goal of the Maven SCM plugin is run, it uses the information in the `scm` tag of the `pom` file to get the SCM details. It uses this information and invokes the corresponding `scm` command to get the status information. In the preceding example, it is the `git status`.

 The command-line version of the relevant SCM client must be installed and available in the Maven path for this to work.

There are three entries in the `scm` tag:

▸ `connection`: This is the connection information to access the repository. This is typically in the following form:

```
<service name>:<scm implementation>:<repository url>
```

   ❑ `service name`: This would be an SCM

   ❑ `scm implementation`: This would be one of the supported SCMs

   ❑ `repository url`: This would be a URL for the repository

▸ `developerConnection`: This is similar to any connection, except that this may need authentication or have additional privileges. Typically, the `connection` access would be read-only, while the `developerConnection` access would be read-write.

▸ `url`: This is the repository URL.

You will also notice that the appropriate shell command is used based on the operating system, which is `cmd.exe` in the case of Windows and `sh` in the case of Linux.

There's more...

The Maven SCM plugin provides a number of other commands for various SCM operations, such as `add`, `remove`, `checkin`, `checkout`, `update`, `diff`, `branch`, and `tag`.

Bootstrap is an interesting option to checkout and build a project with:

1. Create a new Maven project (or open the `bootstrap-project` file).

2. Add a valid Maven project in the `scm` section:

```
scm>
    <connection>scm:git:https://github.com/maruhgar/mvn-examples</connection>
    <url>https://github.com/maruhgar/mvn-examples</url>
</scm>
```

3. Add the following entries in the `build` section:

```
<build>
  <plugins>
    <plugin>
      <groupId>org.apache.maven.plugins</groupId>
      <artifactId>maven-scm-plugin</artifactId>
      <version>1.9.2</version>
      <configuration>
        <goals>install</goals>
        <goalsDirectory>test-properties</goalsDirectory>
      </configuration>
    </plugin>
  </plugins>
</build>
```

4. Run the Maven command:

   mvn scm:bootstrap

5. Observe the results:

```
C:\projects\apache-maven-cookbook\bootstrap-project>mvn scm:bootstrap
[INFO] Scanning for projects...
[INFO]
[INFO]
[INFO] ------------------------------------------------------------------------
[INFO] Building Bootstrap Project 1.0-SNAPSHOT
[INFO] ------------------------------------------------------------------------
[INFO]
[INFO] --- maven-scm-plugin:1.9.2:bootstrap (default-cli) @ bootstratp-project -

[INFO] Removing C:\projects\apache-maven-cookbook\bootstrap-project\target\check
out
[INFO] Executing: cmd.exe /X /C "git clone https://github.com/maruhgar/mvn-examp
les C:\projects\apache-maven-cookbook\bootstrap-project\target\checkout"
[INFO] Working directory: C:\projects\apache-maven-cookbook\bootstrap-project\ta
rget
[INFO] Executing: cmd.exe /X /C "git ls-remote https://github.com/maruhgar/mvn-e
xamples"
[INFO] Working directory: C:\Users\raghu\AppData\Local\Temp
[INFO] Executing: cmd.exe /X /C "git pull https://github.com/maruhgar/mvn-exampl
es master"
[INFO] Working directory: C:\projects\apache-maven-cookbook\bootstrap-project\ta
rget\checkout
[INFO] Executing: cmd.exe /X /C "git checkout"
[INFO] Working directory: C:\projects\apache-maven-cookbook\bootstrap-project\ta
rget\checkout
[INFO] Executing: cmd.exe /X /C "git ls-files"
[INFO] Working directory: C:\projects\apache-maven-cookbook\bootstrap-project\ta
rget\checkout
[INFO] Scanning for projects...
[INFO]
[INFO]
[INFO] ------------------------------------------------------------------------
[INFO] Building test-properties 1.0-SNAPSHOT
[INFO] ------------------------------------------------------------------------
[INFO]
[INFO] --- maven-resources-plugin:2.6:resources (default-resources) @ test-prope
rties ---
[WARNING] Using platform encoding (Cp1252 actually) to copy filtered resources,
i.e. build is platform dependent!
[INFO] skip non existing resourceDirectory C:\projects\apache-maven-cookbook\boo
tstrap-project\target\checkout\test-properties\src\main\resources
[INFO]
```

Our Maven project has checked another Maven project, using the information in the `scm` section, and run the specified goal on this. We specify a `goalsDirectory` element because the SCM contains a number of projects and we want to execute the goals for a specific project, in this case `test-properties`.

Generating changelogs for a site

Now that we have seen the Maven SCM plugin in action, we can see how we can use this feature to generate a log of project changes as part of the site report.

How to do it...

1. Open the Maven project `project-with-documentation`.

2. Add the following entry in the `reporting` section:

   ```xml
   <plugin>
     <groupId>org.apache.maven.plugins</groupId>
     <artifactId>maven-changelog-plugin</artifactId>
     <version>2.3</version>
   </plugin>
   ```

3. Run the following command:

   ```
   mvn site
   ```

4. Observe the output:

   ```
   [INFO] Generating "Change Log" report     --- maven-changelog-
   plugin:2.3

   [INFO] Generating changed sets xml to:
   C:\projects\apache-maven-cookbook\project-with-documentation\
   target\changelog.xml

   [INFO] Executing: cmd.exe /X /C "git whatchanged
   "--since=2014-11-06 02:45:57 +0

   000" "--until=2014-12-07 02:45:57 +0000" --date=iso --
   C:\projects\apache-maven-cookbook\project-with-documentation"
   ```

5. Observe the generated reports:

How it works...

When the `site` command is run, Maven uses the information in the `reporting` section of the `pom` file to generate various reports. It finds an entry for the Maven Changelog plugin and generates the corresponding changelog report.

This is essentially the SCM log for the project, with details such as timestamp, author, and details of change.

Multi-module Projects

9

In this chapter we will cover the following recipes:

- ▶ Understanding project inheritance
- ▶ Understanding project aggregation
- ▶ Combining inheritance and aggregation
- ▶ Performing multi-module dependency management
- ▶ Performing multi-module plugin management
- ▶ Selectively building modules
- ▶ Reporting for multi-module projects

Introduction

Except for simple projects, most real-life projects have more than one module. Each of them can be developed independently. Some modules might depend on others. A project that uses these modules would want to ensure that it builds successfully with the appropriate versions of all the modules.

As we look at multiple modules, each module may use a number of dependencies. To avoid dependency hell, it is important that the versions of dependencies used by each module are managed well. There is also an opportunity to optimize on the dependencies and plugins to reduce the repetition of build scripts.

Understanding project inheritance

There are times when you might want a project to use values from another .pom file. You may be building a large software product, so you do not want to repeat the dependency and other elements multiple times.

Maven provides a feature called **project inheritance** for this. Maven allows a number of elements specified in the parent pom file to be merged to the inheriting project. In fact, the super pom file is an example of project inheritance.

Getting ready

Maven is set up on your system and is verified to work. To do this, refer to *Chapter 1, Getting Started.*

How to do it...

1. Open a project that has inheritance; project-with-inheritance in our case. This has a subfolder named child, which is the project that inherits from the parent.

2. Update the parent pom file as follows:

```
<groupId>com.packt.cookbook</groupId>
<artifactId>project-with-inheritance</artifactId>
<packaging>pom</packaging>
<version>1.0-SNAPSHOT</version>
```

3. Create the pom file for child as follows:

```
<parent>
    <groupId>com.packt.cookbook</groupId>
    <artifactId>project-with-inheritance</artifactId>
    <version>1.0-SNAPSHOT</version>
</parent>
<modelVersion>4.0.0</modelVersion>
<artifactId>child</artifactId>
<packaging>jar</packaging>
<name>Child Project</name>
```

4. Run the following Maven command in the child subfolder:

```
mvn clean package
```

5. Observe the output:

```
C:\projects\apache-maven-cookbook\project-with-inheritance\child>mvn clean packa
ge
[INFO] Scanning for projects...
[INFO]
[INFO] ------------------------------------------------------------------------
[INFO] Building Child Project 1.0-SNAPSHOT
[INFO] ------------------------------------------------------------------------
[INFO]
[INFO] --- maven-clean-plugin:2.5:clean (default-clean) @ child ---
[INFO] Deleting C:\projects\apache-maven-cookbook\project-with-inheritance\child
\target
[INFO]
[INFO] --- maven-resources-plugin:2.6:resources (default-resources) @ child ---
[INFO] Using 'UTF-8' encoding to copy filtered resources.
[INFO] skip non existing resourceDirectory C:\projects\apache-maven-cookbook\pro
ject-with-inheritance\child\src\main\resources
[INFO]
[INFO] --- maven-compiler-plugin:3.1:compile (default-compile) @ child ---
[INFO] Changes detected - recompiling the module!
[INFO] Compiling 1 source file to C:\projects\apache-maven-cookbook\project-with
-inheritance\child\target\classes
```

How it works...

We specified a `parent` element in the pom file of `child`. Here, we added the coordinates of the parent, namely `groupId`, `artifactId`, and `version`. We did not specify the `groupId` and `version` coordinates of the `child` project. We also did not specify any `properties` and `dependencies`.

In the parent pom file, we specified `properties` and `dependencies`.

Due to the relationship defined, when Maven runs on the `child` project, it inherits `groupId`, `version`, `properties`, and `dependencies` defined in the parent.

Interestingly, the parent pom file (`project-with-inheritance`) is oblivious to the fact that there is a `child` project.

However, this only works if the parent project is of the pom type.

How did Maven know where the parent pom is located? We did not specify a location in the pom file. This is because, by default, Maven looks for the parent pom in the parent folder of `child`. Otherwise, it attempts to download the parent pom from the repository.

There's more...

What if the parent pom is not in any repository? Also, what if it is in a different folder from the parent folder of the child? Let's see what happens:

1. Open a child project, where the parent project is not in the `parent` folder but in a subfolder (in our case, `parent`):

```
├──child
│       pom.xml
│
│   └──src
│       ├──main
│       │   └──java
│       │       └──com
│       │           └──packt
│       │               └──cookbook
│       │                   App.java
│       │
│       └──test
│           └──java
│               └──com
│                   └──packt
│                       └──cookbook
│                           AppTest.java
│
└──parent
        pom.xml
```

2. Update the pom file of the child project as follows:

```xml
<parent>
    <groupId>com.packt.cookbook</groupId>
    <artifactId>parent</artifactId>
    <version>1.0-SNAPSHOT</version>
    <relativePath>../parent/pom.xml</relativePath>
</parent>
```

3. Build the `child` project:

```
mvn clean package
```

Maven now determines the location of the parent pom by virtue of the `relativePath` element, which indicates the folder where the parent pom is located. Using this, it builds the child project successfully.

Understanding project aggregation

A key difference between inheritance and aggregation is that, aggregation is defined with a top-down approach, whereas inheritance is defined the other way around. In Maven, project aggregation is similar to project inheritance, except that the change is made in the parent pom instead of the child pom.

Maven uses the term **module** to define a child or subproject, which is part of a larger project. An aggregate project can build all the modules together. Also, a Maven command run on the parent pom or the pom file of the aggregate project will also apply to all the modules that it contains.

How to do it...

1. Open a project that has aggregation; in our case `project-with-aggregation`. This has a subfolder named `aggregate-child`, which is the module that is aggregated by the parent project.

2. Update the parent pom as follows:

   ```
   <groupId>com.packt.cookbook</groupId>
   <artifactId>project-with-aggregation</artifactId>
   <packaging>pom</packaging>
   <version>1.0-SNAPSHOT</version>
   ```

3. Add the `module` section and specify the child:

   ```
   <modules>
       <module>aggregate-child</module>
   </module>
   ```

4. Run the following Maven command in the `parent` folder:

   mvn clean package

5. Observe the output:

   ```
   C:\projects\apache-maven-cookbook\project-with-aggregation>mvn
   clean package

   [INFO] Scanning for projects...
   [INFO] ------------------------------------------------------------
   -------------
   [INFO] Reactor Build Order:
   [INFO]
   [INFO] Aggregate child Project
   ```

```
[INFO] project-with-aggregation

...

[INFO] -----------------------------------------------------------
-------------

[INFO] Reactor Summary:

[INFO]

[INFO] Child Project .......................................
SUCCESS [  2.866 s]

[INFO] project-with-aggregation ...........................
SUCCESS [  0.004 s]

[INFO] -----------------------------------------------------------
-------------

[INFO] BUILD SUCCESS

[INFO] -----------------------------------------------------------
-------------
```

How it works...

We specified the `child` project as a module in the aggregator pom. The child project is a normal Maven project, which has no information about the fact that there exists an aggregator pom.

When the aggregator project is built, it builds the child project in turn. You will notice the word `Reactor` in the Maven output. Reactor is a part of Maven, which allows it to execute a goal on a set of modules. While modules are discrete units of work; they can be gathered together using the reactor to build them simultaneously. The reactor determines the correct build order from the dependencies stated by each module.

There's more...

As in the case of inheritance, what the module is, is not a subfolder of the aggregator project, but a sibling.

1. Update the `module` section as follows:

   ```
   <modules>
       <module>../aggregate-child</module>
   </module>
   ```

2. Build the aggregator project:

   mvn clean package

Maven now determines the location of the module by virtue of the path specified, which indicates the folder where the parent pom is located. By convention, the module name is expected to be identical to the folder name.

Combining inheritance and aggregation

By using the project inheritance feature of Maven, we can share common build attributes such as `properties` and `dependencies` across all children. We can also aggregate modules and build them together.

When project inheritance is used, the parent is not aware of the child. In the case of project aggregation, each module is not aware of the aggregation.

We will now see how to combine and get the benefits of both.

How to do it...

1. Open a multi-module project; in our case, `simple-multi-module`. This has a subfolder `child`, which is the module that is aggregated by the parent project.

2. Update the parent pom as follows:

    ```
    <groupId>com.packt.cookbook</groupId>
    <artifactId>simple-multi-module</artifactId>
    <packaging>pom</packaging>
    <version>1.0-SNAPSHOT</version>
    ```

3. Add the `module` section and specify the child:

    ```
    <modules>
        <module>child</module>
    ```

4. Update the child pom to specify the `parent` element:

    ```
    <parent>
      <groupId>com.packt.cookbook</groupId>
      <artifactId>simple-multi-module</artifactId>
      <version>1.0-SNAPSHOT</version>
    </parent>
    ```

5. Run the following Maven command in the parent folder:

    ```
    mvn clean package
    ```

6. Observe the output:

```
[INFO] Reactor Summary:

[INFO]

[INFO] simple-multi-module ...............................
SUCCESS [  0.162 s]

[INFO] Child Project .....................................
SUCCESS [  2.411 s]
```

How it works...

We have specified the `parent` element in the `child` pom to indicate who the parent is.
We have also specified the `child` project as a module in the parent pom. Thus, both the
relationships—inheritance and aggregation—are defined.

When we build the parent project, it automatically builds the child by virtue of the `modules`
element. At the same time, the child project can be built independently as well.

There's more...

The child project need not necessarily be a subfolder of the parent project. If it is elsewhere,
as we have seen in the earlier recipes, it can be one of the following:

▸   `relativePath`: `relativePath` of the parent element should point to the
    appropriate location of the parent

▸   `module`: The `module` element should contain the appropriate path to the
    child project

Performing multi-module dependency management

Dependency management is a mechanism to centralize dependency information. When there
are a set of projects (or modules) that inherit a common parent, all information about the
dependency can be put in the parent pom and the projects can have simpler references to
them. This makes it easy to maintain the dependencies across multiple projects and reduces
the issues that typically arise due to multiple versions of the same dependencies.

How to do it...

1. Open a multi-module project (simple-multi-module).

2. Add a dependency for junit in the dependencyManagement section:

```
<dependencyManagement>
    <dependencies>
      <dependency>
        <groupId>junit</groupId>
        <artifactId>junit</artifactId>
        <version>3.8.1</version>
        <scope>test</scope>
      </dependency>
    </dependencies>
</dependencyManagement>
```

3. Update the dependencies section of the child project as follows:

```
<dependencies>
    <dependency>
      <groupId>junit</groupId>
      <artifactId>junit</artifactId>
    </dependency>
</dependencies>
```

4. Run the following command:

mvn clean test

Ensure that the build completes successfully.

5. Run the Maven command to check the dependency:

mvn dependency:tree

6. Observe the results:

```
[INFO] --- maven-dependency-plugin:2.8:tree (default-cli) @
simple-multi-module

---

[INFO] com.packt.cookbook:simple-multi-module:pom:1.0-SNAPSHOT

[INFO]

[INFO] -----------------------------------------------------------
-------------

[INFO] Building Child Project 1.0-SNAPSHOT

[INFO] -----------------------------------------------------------
-------------
```

```
[INFO]
[INFO] --- maven-dependency-plugin:2.8:tree (default-cli) @ child
---
[INFO] com.packt.cookbook:child:jar:1.0-SNAPSHOT
[INFO] \- junit:junit:jar:3.8.1:test
```

How it works...

Dependencies that are specified within the `dependencyManagement` section of the parent pom are available for use to all the child projects. The child project needs to choose the dependencies by explicitly specifying the required dependencies in the `dependencies` section. While doing this, the child projects can omit the `version` and `scope` information so that they are inherited from the parent.

You may ask, "Why have the `dependencyManagement` section when child projects inherit dependencies defined in the parent pom anyway?" The reason is, the parent centralizes dependencies across several projects. A child project typically needs only some of the dependencies that the parent defines and not all of them. The `dependencyManagement` section allows child projects to selectively choose these.

There's more...

The `dependencyManagement` section also helps address any surprises of Maven's dependency mediation. Dependency mediation is what determines what version of dependency will be used when multiple versions of an artifact are encountered. However, `dependencyManagement` takes precedence over dependency mediation and ensures that dependency mediation does not pick a version over the one specified in `dependencyManagement`.

It should be noted that dependencies on different versions are error prone and `dependencyManagement` cannot always save them from library version incompatibilities.

Performing multi-module plugin management

In multi-module projects, `pluginManagement` allows you to configure plugin information that can be used as required by child projects. The parent pom can define the configurations for various plugins used by different child projects. Each child project can chose the plugins that it needs for the build.

How to do it...

1. Open a multi-module project (`simple-multi-module`).

2. Add a configuration for the Maven build helper plugin in the `pluginManagement` section to copy additional resources:

```xml
<pluginManagement>
  <plugins>
   <plugin>
     <groupId>org.codehaus.mojo</groupId>
     <artifactId>build-helper-maven-plugin</artifactId>
     <version>1.9.1</version>
     <executions>
       <execution>
         <id>add-resource</id>
         <phase>generate-resources</phase>
         <goals>
           <goal>add-resource</goal>
         </goals>
         <configuration>
           <resources>
             <resource>
               <directory>src/resources/xml</directory>
               <targetPath>xml</targetPath>
             </resource>
             <resource>
               <directory>src/resources/json</directory>
               <targetPath>json</targetPath>
                 <includes>
                   <include>include.json</include>
                 </includes>
                 <excludes>
                   <exclude>exclude.json</exclude>
                 </excludes>
             </resource>
           </resources>
         </configuration>
       </execution>
     </executions>
   </plugin>
  </plugins>
 </pluginManagement>
</build>
```

3. Run the following command to build the project:

```
mvn clean test
```

Note that the additional resources are not getting copied in the child project.

4. Now, use the corresponding plugin in the child project:

```
<build>
    <plugins>
        <plugin>
            <groupId>org.codehaus.mojo</groupId>
            <artifactId>build-helper-maven-plugin</artifactId>
        </plugin>
    </plugins>
</build>
```

5. Build the project again.

6. Observe the output:

```
[INFO] Copying 2 resources to xml
[INFO] Copying 1 resource to json
```

How it works...

We defined the Maven build helper plugin to copy resources from additional folders in the `pluginManagement` section of the parent pom. It is not available to the child pom until the child uses the plugin. When the child project did not define the plugin, the plugin definition in the parent pom had no effect. When the child project defined the plugin, it took effect and the additional resources got copied over.

There's more...

If a plugin is used as part of the build lifecycle, then its configuration in the `pluginManagement` section will take effect, even if not explicitly defined by the child. Let us see how this happens:

1. Define the Maven compiler plugin in `pluginManagement` of the parent pom:

```
<pluginManagement>
    <plugins>
        <plugin>
            <groupId>org.apache.maven.plugins</groupId>
            <artifactId>maven-compiler-plugin</artifactId>
            <version>3.2</version>
            <configuration>
```

```
            <source>1.8</source>
            <target>1.8</target>
         </configuration>
       </plugin>
     <plugin>
</pluginManagement>
```

2. Without adding the plugin to the child pom, run the following command using Java 7:

   mvn clean test

3. Observe the error:

   [ERROR] Failed to execute goal org.apache.maven.plugins:maven-compiler-plugin:3.

   2:compile (default-compile) on project child: Fatal error compiling: invalid tar

   get release: 1.8 -> [Help 1]

What happened here? Even though the child pom did not define the Maven Compiler plugin, the configuration for the Maven Compiler plugin in the `pluginManagement` section of the parent pom took effect because the `compile` goal was part of the build lifecycle. As the configuration stipulated a Java 8 target, the compilation failed.

What if we do not want to inherit specific plugin configurations? Maven provides a way to do this. Let us see how:

1. Update the preceding Maven Compiler plugin configuration as follows:

   ```
   <pluginManagement>
        <plugins>
          <plugin>
              <groupId>org.apache.maven.plugins</groupId>
              <artifactId>maven-compiler-plugin</artifactId>
              <version>3.2</version>
              <inherited>false</inherited>
              <configuration>
                <source>1.8</source>
                <target>1.8</target>
              </configuration>
          </plugin>
        <plugin>
   </pluginManagement>
   ```

2. Now run the following using Java 7:

   mvn clean package

3. Observe that the project compiles without errors, though the plugin configuration specified Java 8.

This is because the configuration was not inherited to the child module as we set the `inherited` element to `false`.

Selectively building modules

When a project has a number of modules, there may be situations when we might want to selectively build modules. One such situation could be because the module might run only on specific machines. Another reason could be that a module may have long-running tests that may make sense only in test servers.

Let us see how we can selectively build modules by using the **profile** feature of Maven.

How to do it...

1. Open a multi-module project that has two modules (`two-multi-module`), namely `common-one` and `dev-two`.

2. In the parent pom, add one project to the `modules` section:

```
<modules>
    <module>common-one</module>
</modules>
```

3. Define a profile and include both modules:

```
<profiles>
    <profile>
        <id>dev</id>
        <modules>
            <module>common-one</module>
            <module>dev-two</module>
        </modules>
    </profile>
</profiles>
```

4. Run the Maven command to build with the `dev` profile:

mvn -P dev clean test

5. Observe the result:

```
[INFO] -------------------------------------------------------------
[INFO] Reactor Summary:
[INFO]
[INFO] two-multi-module ............................... SUCCESS [  0.144 s]
[INFO] First Child Project ............................ SUCCESS [  1.980 s]
[INFO] Second Child Project ........................... SUCCESS [  0.334 s]
[INFO] -------------------------------------------------------------
[INFO] BUILD SUCCESS
[INFO] -------------------------------------------------------------
```

6. Run the Maven command to build without profile:

   mvn clean test

7. Observe the result:

```
[INFO] -------------------------------------------------------------
[INFO] Reactor Summary:
[INFO]
[INFO] two-multi-module ............................... SUCCESS [  0.164 s]
[INFO] First Child Project ............................ SUCCESS [  2.108 s]
[INFO]
```

How it works...

When you have multiple modules and you want to control when specific ones should be built, the simplest way to achieve this is to define specific profiles and define modules within each of them. In our example, we created a `dev` profile to build both modules, `common-one` and `dev-two`. The default Maven build builds only the `common-one` module.

What we achieved is the ability to exclude or skip specific modules from build as required. As you saw, a profile can only extend the list of modules, so it cannot actually blacklist a module.

> Similarly, we could define `pluginManagement` and `dependencyManagement` within profiles so that these take effect only for the profiles.

There's more...

Maven also provides command-line options to build modules selectively. Here are some of them with examples based on the `two-multi-module` Maven project:

▶ `-pl -projects`: This is a comma-separated list of projects to be built. An example for this is as follows:

   mvn clean package -pl common-one

- ► -am: This stands for --also-make: This builds projects required by the list if the project list is specified:

```
mvn clean package -pl common-one -am
```

- ► -amd: This stands for --also-make-dependants. This builds projects that depend on projects on the list (if project list is specified):

```
mvn clean package -pl common-one -amd
```

- ► -rf: This stands for -resume-from. This resumes build from a specific project (useful in the case of failures in a multi-module build):

```
mvn -Pdev clean package -rf dev-two
```

Reporting for multi-module projects

When we talk about generating a site report for a multi-module project, we refer to generating this for each module of the project and the parent project. In the case of the site report for a multi-module project, a couple of factors need to be taken into account. The first one is to test if the links between the parent and the modules work correctly. The other is to check if certain site reports can be aggregated instead of being reported individually for each module.

How to do it...

1. Open a multi-module project (two-multi-module) with two modules, one and two.
2. Add the following command to the reporting section of the parent pom for checkstyle:

```xml
<plugin>
    <groupId>org.apache.maven.plugins</groupId>
    <artifactId>maven-checkstyle-plugin</artifactId>
    <version>2.13</version>
    <reportSets>
      <reportSet>
        <id>aggregate</id>
        <inherited>false</inherited>
        <reports>
          <report>checkstyle-aggregate</report>
        </reports>
      </reportSet>
    </reportSets>
</plugin>
```

3. Run the command to generate site report:

   `mvn test site`

4. Click on the **Checkstyle** link in the site report:

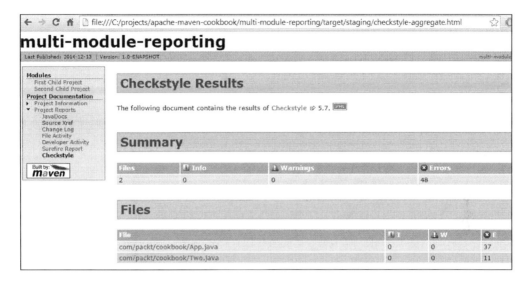

How it works...

When the `site` goal is run for a multi-module project, it generates the site report for all the modules in addition to the parent module. All the reports are separately generated for each module. However, plugins such as Checkstyle provide an option to generate aggregated report across all the modules of the project. This allows us to get a consolidated view of the Checkstyle violations across all the modules of the project.

> Other reporting plugins such as FindBugs, PMD, and Cobertura support multi-module reporting. However, not all of them support the aggregation of reports. Other reporting plugins that allow aggregated reporting are Javadocs and JXR.

There's more...

Though the site report generated for a multi-module project includes links to each child module, the links will not work correctly, as each module report is in the `target/site` folder of the respective module.

Let's see how we can verify that the modules are correctly linked in the report:

1. Add a `distributionManagement` section in the parent pom:

```
<distributionManagement>
    <site>
      <id>packt</id>
      <url>file:///C:/fullsite</url>
    </site>
  </distributionManagement>
```

2. Run the following command to generate site report:

mvn test site

3. Run the following command to stage the site:

mvn site:stage –DstagingDirectory=C:/fullsite

4. Open the folder:

Local Disk (C:) ▸ fullsite			∨ ⏿	Search fullsite
Name	Date modified	Type	Size	
apidocs	13-12-2014 17:51	File folder		
css	13-12-2014 17:51	File folder		
images	13-12-2014 17:51	File folder		
one	13-12-2014 17:51	File folder		
two	13-12-2014 17:51	File folder		
xref	13-12-2014 17:51	File folder		
changelog	13-12-2014 17:51	Chrome HTML Do...	6 KB	
checkstyle	13-12-2014 17:51	RSS File	3 KB	
checkstyle-aggregate	13-12-2014 17:51	Chrome HTML Do...	21 KB	
dependencies	13-12-2014 17:51	Chrome HTML Do...	7 KB	
dependency-convergence	13-12-2014 17:51	Chrome HTML Do...	8 KB	
dependency-info	13-12-2014 17:51	Chrome HTML Do...	8 KB	
dependency-management	13-12-2014 17:51	Chrome HTML Do...	7 KB	
dev-activity	13-12-2014 17:51	Chrome HTML Do...	6 KB	
distribution-management	13-12-2014 17:51	Chrome HTML Do...	7 KB	
file-activity	13-12-2014 17:51	Chrome HTML Do...	6 KB	
index	13-12-2014 17:51	Chrome HTML Do...	7 KB	
integration	13-12-2014 17:51	Chrome HTML Do...	7 KB	
issue-tracking	13-12-2014 17:51	Chrome HTML Do...	7 KB	
license	13-12-2014 17:51	Chrome HTML Do...	10 KB	

You will notice that the site data for both the modules are now subfolders of the project site folder. Opening the index page of `fullsite` will allow us to navigate to each module site and ensure that the links are working:

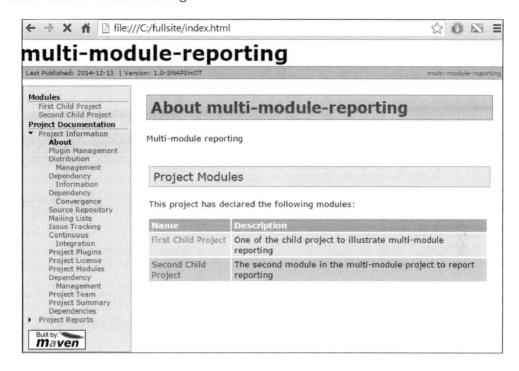

10

Java Development with Maven

In this chapter, we will cover the following recipes:

- ▶ Building a JAR project
- ▶ Generating an executable JAR
- ▶ Generating a JAR of the source code
- ▶ Generating a JAR of the test classes
- ▶ Building a WAR project
- ▶ Building an EAR project
- ▶ Building a pom project
- ▶ Running a web project with Jetty
- ▶ Running a web project with Tomcat

Introduction

Maven is primarily a build tool for Java projects. Java projects can generate different types of binaries. Typically, the output of a Java project is a JAR file. For web applications, Java classes combined with other type of files result in a WAR or EAR file as well. Maven provides plugins and lifecycle phases to generate various types of binary artifacts for Java projects.

Building a JAR project

The default type of artifact generated by Maven is JAR. If the `packaging` element is absent, or specified as `jar`, Maven considers it a JAR project. A JAR project combines all the source classes along with the necessary project resources to a single file. This JAR file can be distributed for it to be used elsewhere.

Getting ready

Maven is set up on your system and is verified for work. To do this, refer to *Chapter 1, Getting Started*.

How to do it...

1. Open a simple Maven project, in our case `simple-project`.

2. Verify that the type is absent or set to `jar`:

   ```
   <modelVersion>4.0.0</modelVersion>
   <groupId>com.packt.cookbook</groupId>
   <artifactId>simple-project</artifactId>
   <packaging>jar</packaging>
   ```

3. Run the following Maven command:

   ```
   mvn clean package
   ```

4. Observe the output:

   ```
   [INFO] --- maven-jar-plugin:2.4:jar (default-jar) @ simple-project
   ---

   [INFO] Building jar: C:\Users\Deepa\Documents\apache-maven-
   cookbook\simple-project\target\simple-project-1.0-SNAPSHOT.jar
   ```

How it works...

The `package` option is part of Maven's default lifecycle. When Maven is run with the `package` option, it runs all the phases up to and prior to it, in order. Maven first compiles the project, runs the tests, and then, based on the packaging type, invokes the suitable plugin to package. In our case, as we specified the packaging as `jar`, Maven used the `jar` goal of the Maven JAR plugin to create a JAR artifact in the `target` folder.

▶ The *Generating an executable JAR* recipe in this chapter

Generating an executable JAR

The JAR artifact generated by Maven works well when used as a dependency in another project. However, it cannot be run as an executable without manually specifying the main class and explicitly specifying the dependencies that the project uses in the classpath.

What if we want to create an executable JAR for the project? This may be useful when the JAR needs to be tested or the project is a simple tool that should be invoked without additional effort.

How to do it...

1. Open a simple Maven project (`project-with-executable-jar`):

2. Add the following section in the `pom` file:

```
<build>
    <plugins>
      <plugin>
        <groupId>org.apache.maven.plugins</groupId>
        <artifactId>maven-jar-plugin</artifactId>
        <version>2.6</version>
        <configuration>
          <archive>
            <manifest>
              <addClasspath>true</addClasspath>
              <mainClass>com.packt.cookbook.App</mainClass>
            </manifest>
          </archive>
        </configuration>
      </plugin>
    </plugins>
  </build>
```

3. Add the plugin configuration to copy over the dependencies to the `target` folder:

```
<plugin>
        <groupId>org.apache.maven.plugins</groupId>
        <artifactId>maven-dependency-plugin</artifactId>
        <version>2.9</version>
        <executions>
```

```
      <execution>
        <id>copy-dependencies</id>
        <phase>package</phase>
        <goals>
          <goal>copy-dependencies</goal>
        </goals>
        <configuration>
        <outputDirectory>${project.build.directory}</
outputDirectory>
          <excludeArtifactIds>junit</excludeArtifactIds>
        </configuration>
      </execution>
    </executions>
  </plugin>
```

4. Run the following command:

    mvn clean package

5. Observe the `target` folder:

```
C:\projects\apache-maven-cookbook\project-with-executable-jar>dir target
 Volume in drive C has no label.
 Volume Serial Number is 04B8-E184

 Directory of C:\projects\apache-maven-cookbook\project-with-executable-jar\targ
et

18-12-2014  06:35    <DIR>          .
18-12-2014  06:35    <DIR>          ..
18-12-2014  06:35    <DIR>          classes
18-12-2014  06:35           270,750 logback-classic-1.1.2.jar
18-12-2014  06:35           427,729 logback-core-1.1.2.jar
18-12-2014  06:35    <DIR>          maven-archiver
18-12-2014  06:35    <DIR>          maven-status
18-12-2014  06:35             3,036 project-with-executable-jar-1.0-SNAPSHOT.jar

18-12-2014  06:35            32,121 slf4j-api-1.7.9.jar
18-12-2014  06:35    <DIR>          surefire-reports
18-12-2014  06:35    <DIR>          test-classes
```

6. Run the generated JAR file:

    java -jar project-with-executable-jar-1.0-SNAPSHOT.jar

7. Observe the output:

    C:\projects\apache-maven-cookbook\project-with-executable-
    jar\target>java -jar project-with-executable-jar-1.0-
    SNAPSHOT.jar

    06:40:18.437 [main] INFO com.packt.cookbook.App - Hello World

How it works...

We have made the following configurations to the Maven JAR plugin in our pom file:

> ▶ **Added classpath**: This adds all the dependant JARs to the manifest classpath section
>
> ▶ **Specified the main class**: This information is again updated in the manifest

We also added the `copy-dependencies` goal of the Maven Dependency plugin to copy over the required dependencies to the folder where the executable JAR is generated.

When we then run the executable JAR, it uses the manifest file to determine the main class as well as the dependencies, loads them, and runs.

Let us look at the manifest file generated:

```
Manifest-Version: 1.0
Built-By: raghu
Build-Jdk: 1.7.0_67
Class-Path: slf4j-api-1.7.9.jar logback-classic-1.1.2.jar logback-core
 -1.1.2.jar
Created-By: Apache Maven 3.2.3
Main-Class: com.packt.cookbook.App
Archiver-Version: Plexus Archiver
```

Evidently, for this to work, the executable JAR should be accompanied by the dependencies that it uses. In the *Creating an assembly* recipe in *Chapter 11, Advanced Maven Usage*, we will learn how to create an assembly with all the dependencies, which can be distributed more easily.

Generating a JAR of the source code

For many projects, it is useful to generate a JAR of the source code along with the artifact. The source thus generated can be imported to IDEs and used for browsing and debugging. Typically, the artifacts of most open source projects are accompanied by sources and Javadocs.

How to do it...

1. Open a project for which you want to generate and attach the source code (`project-with-source-code`).

2. Add the following plugin configuration to the pom file:

```
<build>
  <plugins>
```

```
<plugin>
  <groupId>org.apache.maven.plugins</groupId>
  <artifactId>maven-source-plugin</artifactId>
  <version>2.4</version>
  <executions>
    <execution>
      <id>attach-sources</id>
      <phase>package</phase>
      <goals>
        <goal>jar-no-fork</goal>
      </goals>
    </execution>
  </executions>
</plugin>
      </plugins>
    </build>
```

3. Run the following Maven command:

```
mvn clean package
```

4. Observe the output:

```
[INFO] --- maven-jar-plugin:2.4:jar (default-jar) @ project-with-
source-attached ---

[INFO] Building jar: C:\projects\apache-maven-cookbook\project-
with-source-attached\target\project-with-source-attached-1.0-
SNAPSHOT.jar

[INFO]

[INFO] --- maven-source-plugin:2.4:jar-no-fork (attach-sources) @
project-with-source-attached ---

[INFO] Building jar: C:\projects\apache-maven-cookbook\project-
with-source-attached\target\project-with-source-attached-1.0-
SNAPSHOT-sources.jar

[INFO] ------------------------------------------------------------
-------------

[INFO] BUILD SUCCESS

[INFO] ------------------------------------------------------------
-----------
```

5. Examine the `target` folder:

```
 Directory of C:\projects\apache-maven-cookbook\project-with-source-attached\tar
get
18-12-2014  09:40    <DIR>          .
18-12-2014  09:40    <DIR>          ..
18-12-2014  09:40    <DIR>          classes
18-12-2014  09:40    <DIR>          maven-archiver
18-12-2014  09:39    <DIR>          maven-status
18-12-2014  09:40               942 project-with-source-attached-1.0-SNAPSHOT-so
urces.jar
18-12-2014  09:40             2,599 project-with-source-attached-1.0-SNAPSHOT.ja
r
18-12-2014  09:40    <DIR>          surefire-reports
18-12-2014  09:40    <DIR>          test-classes
```

How it works...

We added the Maven Source plugin to the `pom` file. We also configured the plugin to run the `jar-no-fork` goal during the package phase. The goal creates a JAR of the project source code and makes it available along with the project artifacts.

The `jar-no-fork` goal is used to bind the goal to the build lifecycle. To run the plugin and create the JAR independent of the lifecycle, the `jar` goal can be used as follows:

```
mvn source:jar
```

Subsequent phases (such as `install`) install the source artifact along with the project artifact.

There's more...

What if we want to attach the Javadoc instead of (or in addition to) sources? Let us do this:

1. Add the following plugin to the `pom` file:

```
<plugin>
    <groupId>org.apache.maven.plugins</groupId>
    <artifactId>maven-javadoc-plugin</artifactId>
    <version>2.10.1</version>
    <executions>
      <execution>
        <id>attach-javadocs</id>
        <phase>package</phase>
        <goals>
          <goal>jar</goal>
        </goals>
      </execution>
    </executions>
</plugin>
```

2. Build the aggregator project:

   mvn clean package

3. Observe the output:

```
[INFO] --- maven-jar-plugin:2.4:jar (default-jar) @ project-with-source-attached
---
[INFO] Building jar: C:\projects\apache-maven-cookbook\project-with-source-attac
hed\target\project-with-source-attached-1.0-SNAPSHOT.jar
[INFO]
[INFO] --- maven-source-plugin:2.4:jar-no-fork (attach-sources) @ project-with-s
ource-attached ---
[INFO] Building jar: C:\projects\apache-maven-cookbook\project-with-source-attac
hed\target\project-with-source-attached-1.0-SNAPSHOT-sources.jar
[INFO]
[INFO] --- maven-javadoc-plugin:2.10.1:jar (attach-javadocs) @ project-with-sour
ce-attached ---
[INFO]
Loading source files for package com.packt.cookbook...
Constructing Javadoc information...
Standard Doclet version 1.7.0_67
Building tree for all the packages and classes...
Generating C:\projects\apache-maven-cookbook\project-with-source-attached\target
\apidocs\com\packt\cookbook\App.html...
Generating C:\projects\apache-maven-cookbook\project-with-source-attached\target
\apidocs\com\packt\cookbook\package-frame.html...
```

Maven runs the `jar` goal of the Maven Javadoc plugin in addition to the `jar-no-fork` goal of the Maven Source plugin. Both the JARs are now created, in addition to the project artifacts, and are now available for distribution.

 Besides sources, the test sources and test Javadocs can also be generated and attached, if relevant to the project.

Generating a JAR of the test classes

There could be situations when you would want to use the test classes and resources of a project as a test dependency in another project. This is typically the case in multi-module projects, where a module depends on another module. There could be utility code in the test classes of a module that can be reused in another module.

One way to achieve this would be by creating a separate project to hold these classes. However, that is cumbersome and may be confusing as well.

Maven provides another way to achieve this.

How to do it...

1. Open a project for which you want to create a test JAR (`project-with-test-jar`).

2. Add the following plugin configuration to the pom file:

```
<build>
  <plugins>
    <plugin>
      <groupId>org.apache.maven.plugins</groupId>
      <artifactId>maven-jar-plugin</artifactId>
      <version>2.5</version>
      <executions>
        <execution>
          <goals>
            <goal>test-jar</goal>
          </goals>
        </execution>
      </executions>
    </plugin>
  </plugins>
</build>
```

3. Run the following Maven command:

```
mvn clean package
```

4. Observe the output:

```
[INFO] --- maven-jar-plugin:2.5:jar (default-jar) @ project-with-
test-jar ---

[INFO] Building jar: C:\projects\apache-maven-cookbook\project-
with-test-jar\tar

get\project-with-test-jar-1.0-SNAPSHOT.jar

[INFO]

[INFO] --- maven-jar-plugin:2.5:test-jar (default) @ project-with-
test-jar ---

[INFO] Building jar: C:\projects\apache-maven-cookbook\project-
with-test-jar\tar

get\project-with-test-jar-1.0-SNAPSHOT-tests.jar
```

5. Examine the `target` folder:

```
Directory of C:\projects\apache-maven-cookbook\project-with-test-jar\target

18-12-2014  10:09    <DIR>          .
18-12-2014  10:09    <DIR>          ..
18-12-2014  10:09    <DIR>          classes
18-12-2014  10:09    <DIR>          maven-archiver
18-12-2014  10:09    <DIR>          maven-status
18-12-2014  10:09             2,655 project-with-test-jar-1.0-SNAPSHOT-tests.jar

18-12-2014  10:09             2,619 project-with-test-jar-1.0-SNAPSHOT.jar
18-12-2014  10:09    <DIR>          surefire-reports
18-12-2014  10:09    <DIR>          test-classes
```

How it works...

We specified a `test-jar` goal to the Maven JAR plugin. This asks Maven to generate a JAR of test classes and resources. This JAR can be installed along with the project artifact. It can also be specified as a dependency in another project as follows:

```xml
<dependencies>
  <dependency>
    <groupId>com.packt.cookbook</groupId>
    <artifactId>project-with-test-jar</artifactId>
    <version>1.0-SNAPSHOT</version>
    <type>test-jar</type>
    <scope>test</scope>
  </dependency>
</dependencies>
```

 One thing to note though is the test JAR does not bring its transitive test-scoped dependencies with it if you add a dependency on this. These dependencies, if required, need to be specified by hand.

Building a WAR project

So far, we have been building projects that generate a JAR artifact. When it comes to web applications, we typically create WAR artifacts. Maven supports the building of WAR artifacts. The packaging type `.war` indicates to Maven that it is a WAR artifact. Maven automatically invokes the corresponding lifecycle bindings.

How to do it...

1. Run the following command from the command prompt:

    ```
    mvn archetype:generate –DinteractiveMode=false
    -DgroupId=com.packt.cookbook -DartifactId=simple-webapp
    -DarchetypeArtifactId=maven-archetype-webapp
    ```

2. Observe the output:

    ```
    [INFO] -----------------------------------------------------------------------
    [INFO] Using following parameters for creating project from Old (1.x) Archetype:
    maven-archetype-webapp:1.0
    [INFO] -----------------------------------------------------------------------
    [INFO] Parameter: groupId, Value: com.packt.cookbook
    [INFO] Parameter: packageName, Value: com.packt.cookbook
    [INFO] Parameter: package, Value: com.packt.cookbook
    [INFO] Parameter: artifactId, Value: simple-webapp
    [INFO] Parameter: basedir, Value: C:\projects
    [INFO] Parameter: version, Value: 1.0-SNAPSHOT
    [INFO] project created from Old (1.x) Archetype in dir: C:\projects\simple-webapp
    [INFO] -----------------------------------------------------------------------
    [INFO] BUILD SUCCESS
    [INFO] -----------------------------------------------------------------------
    ```

3. Open the created pom file:

    ```
    <modelVersion>4.0.0</modelVersion>
        <groupId>com.packt.cookbook</groupId>
        <artifactId>simple-webapp</artifactId>
        <packaging>war</packaging>
        <version>1.0-SNAPSHOT</version>
        <name>simple-webapp Maven Webapp</name>
        <url>http://maven.apache.org</url>
        <build>
          <finalName>simple-webapp</finalName>
        </build>
    ```

4. Run the command to build the project:

    ```
    mvn clean package
    ```

5. Observe the output:

```
[INFO]
[INFO] --- maven-war-plugin:2.2:war (default-war) @ simple-webapp ---
[INFO] Packaging webapp
[INFO] Assembling webapp [simple-webapp] in [C:\projects\apache-maven-cookbook\s
imple-webapp\target\simple-webapp]
[INFO] Processing war project
[INFO] Copying webapp resources [C:\projects\apache-maven-cookbook\simple-webapp
\src\main\webapp]
[INFO] Webapp assembled in [35 msecs]
[INFO] Building war: C:\projects\apache-maven-cookbook\simple-webapp\target\simp
le-webapp.war
[INFO] WEB-INF\web.xml already added, skipping
[INFO]
```

6. Check the `target` folder:

```
[Directory of C:\projects\apache-maven-cookbook\simple-webapp\
target

18-12-2014  20:52    <DIR>          .
18-12-2014  20:52    <DIR>          ..
18-12-2014  20:52    <DIR>          classes
18-12-2014  20:52    <DIR>          maven-archiver
18-12-2014  20:52    <DIR>          simple-webapp
18-12-2014  20:52            2,226 simple-webapp.war
```

How it works...

We used the Maven Archetype plugin to bootstrap a simple web project. This generated a pom file along with other contents for a web application. When you examine the pom file, you will notice that the packaging type is set to war.

Maven uses this information to invoke the war goal of the Maven plugin to create a WAR of the project contents.

Also, observe that we specified the finalName element. Maven uses this to create the name of the WAR artifact. In the absence of this element, Maven uses the default name, which would have been simple-webapp-1.0-SNAPSHOT.war.

There's more...

The Maven WAR plugin can be used in many ways. The default option creates a WAR file. During development, we would want to speed up things by generating the WAR file in exploded form. To do this, perform the following steps:

1. Open the simple-webapp project.

2. Run the following command:

   mvn war:exploded

3. Examine the content of the `target` folder:

```
C:\projects\apache-maven-cookbook\simple-webapp\target>tree /f simple-webapp
Folder PATH listing
Volume serial number is 04B8-E184
C:\PROJECTS\APACHE-MAVEN-COOKBOOK\SIMPLE-WEBAPP\TARGET\SIMPLE-WEBAPP
    index.jsp
    maven-feather.png

├───META-INF
└───WEB-INF
        web.xml

    ├───classes
    │   └───com
    │       └───packt
    │           └───cookbook
    │                   App.class

    └───lib
            logback-classic-1.1.2.jar
            logback-core-1.1.2.jar
            slf4j-api-1.7.9.jar
```

Building an EAR project

Maven provides support to generate Java **EE Enterprise Archive** (**EAR**) files. These can be deployed in application servers such as JBoss, WebLogic, and WebSphere.

How to do it...

1. Run the following command from the command prompt:

   ```
   mvn archetype:generate -DgroupId=com.packt.cookbook
   -DartifactId=simple-ear -DarchetypeArtifactId=wildfly-javaee7-
   webapp-ear-archetype -DarchetypeGroupId=org.wildfly.archetype
   -DinteractiveMode=false
   ```

2. Observe the result:

```
[INFO] Using following parameters for creating project from Archetype: wildfly-j
avaee7-webapp-ear-archetype:8.2.0.Final
[INFO] --------------------------------------------------------------------------
[INFO] Parameter: groupId, Value: com.packt.cookbook
[INFO] Parameter: artifactId, Value: simple-ear
[INFO] Parameter: version, Value: 1.0-SNAPSHOT
[INFO] Parameter: package, Value: com.packt.cookbook
[INFO] Parameter: packageInPathFormat, Value: com/packt/cookbook
[INFO] Parameter: version, Value: 1.0-SNAPSHOT
[INFO] Parameter: package, Value: com.packt.cookbook
[INFO] Parameter: groupId, Value: com.packt.cookbook
[INFO] Parameter: artifactId, Value: simple-ear
[INFO] Parent element not overwritten in C:\projects\simple-ear\simple-ear-ejb\p
om.xml
[INFO] Parent element not overwritten in C:\projects\simple-ear\simple-ear-web\p
om.xml
[WARNING] CP Don't override file C:\projects\simple-ear\simple-ear-web\src\main\
webapp\WEB-INF\templates\default.xhtml
[INFO] Parent element not overwritten in C:\projects\simple-ear\simple-ear-ear\p
om.xml
[INFO] project created from Archetype in dir: C:\projects\simple-ear
[INFO] --------------------------------------------------------------------------
[INFO] BUILD SUCCESS
[INFO] --------------------------------------------------------------------------
```

3. Build the generated project:

   mvn clean package

4. Observe the generated output:

```
[INFO] --------------------------------------------------------------------------
[INFO]
[INFO] Reactor Summary:
[INFO]
[INFO] simple-ear ................................................ SUCCESS [  0.164 s]
[INFO] simple-ear: EJB Module .................................... SUCCESS [  5.099 s]
[INFO] simple-ear: WAR Module .................................... SUCCESS [  2.114 s]
[INFO] simple-ear: EAR Module .................................... SUCCESS [  0.887 s]
[INFO]
[INFO] BUILD SUCCESS
[INFO]
```

5. Open the target folder:

How it works...

We used the Maven Archetype plugin to bootstrap a simple EAR project. It generated a multi-module project, which has an EJB module, web module, and a EAR module along with the aggregate pom file. When you examine the pom file of the EAR module, you will notice that the packaging type is set to ear.

Once built, Maven builds all the modules. In the EAR module, it uses the packaging information to invoke the ear goal of the Maven EAR plugin to create a EAR of the project contents.

Building a pom project

There are many reasons why you may want to make a pom file available as an artifact. One reason is the aggregate project. An aggregate project must have the pom packaging type. Another reason could be a pom, which can be imported as a dependency. Whatever the reason, Maven provides support to build a pom project.

How to do it...

1. Open a simple pom project (simple-pom-project).

2. Observe the packaging type:

```
<groupId>com.packt.cookbook</groupId>
    <artifactId>simple-pom-project</artifactId>
    <packaging>pom</packaging>
    <version>1.0-SNAPSHOT</version>
    <description>Simple pom project</description>
```

3. Build the project:

   mvn clean package

   Note that only the clean goal is run.

4. Run the following command:

   mvn clean install

5. Observe the output:

```
C:\projects\apache-maven-cookbook\simple-pom-project>mvn install
[INFO] Scanning for projects...
[INFO]
[INFO] ------------------------------------------------------------------------
[INFO] Building Simple Pom Project 1.0-SNAPSHOT
[INFO] ------------------------------------------------------------------------
[INFO]
[INFO] --- maven-install-plugin:2.4:install (default-install) @ simple-pom-proje
ct
[INFO] Installing C:\projects\apache-maven-cookbook\simple-pom-project\pom.xml t
o C:\software\maven\com\packt\cookbook\simple-pom-project\1.0-SNAPSHOT\simple-po
m-project-1.0-SNAPSHOT.pom
[INFO] ------------------------------------------------------------------------
[INFO] BUILD SUCCESS
[INFO] ------------------------------------------------------------------------
```

How it works...

The following are the default bindings for the pom packaging type:

- ▶ `package: site:attach-descriptor`: This attaches a descriptor to the site report, if applicable
- ▶ `install: install:install`: This installs the project in the local repository
- ▶ `deploy: deploy:deploy`: This deploys the project to the remote repository

As we can see, Maven does not run any other goals for the pom packaging type. However, if it sees module elements, it invokes the specified Maven goals on all the defined modules.

Also, various configurations, including pluginManagement and dependencyManagement, get inherited by all of the child projects.

There's more...

What if you had a reason to compile some source files or run some tests even though the packaging type is pom? This may not be a usual scenario, but it can be done by explicitly invoking the relevant plugin goals in the following way:

1. Open the simple pom project (simple-pom-project).

2. Run the following command:

```
mvn clean compiler:compile compiler:testCompile surefire:test
jar:jar
```

3. Observe the output:

```
C:\projects\apache-maven-cookbook\simple-pom-project>mvn compiler:compile compil
er:testCompile surefire:test jar:jar
[INFO] Scanning for projects...
[INFO]
[INFO] ------------------------------------------------------------------------
[INFO] Building Simple Pom Project 1.0-SNAPSHOT
[INFO] ------------------------------------------------------------------------
[INFO]
[INFO] --- maven-compiler-plugin:3.1:compile (default-cli) @ simple-pom-project
[INFO] Changes detected - recompiling the module!
[INFO] Compiling 1 source file to C:\projects\apache-maven-cookbook\simple-pom-p
roject\target\classes
[INFO]
[INFO] --- maven-compiler-plugin:3.1:testCompile (default-cli) @ simple-pom-proj
ect ---
[INFO] Changes detected - recompiling the module!
[INFO] Compiling 1 source file to C:\projects\apache-maven-cookbook\simple-pom-p
roject\target\test-classes
[INFO]
[INFO] --- maven-surefire-plugin:2.14.1:test (default-cli) @ simple-pom-project

[INFO] Surefire report directory: C:\projects\apache-maven-cookbook\simple-pom-p
roject\target\surefire-reports

-------------------------------------------------------
 T E S T S
-------------------------------------------------------
Running com.packt.cookbook.AppTest
Tests run: 1, Failures: 0, Errors: 0, Skipped: 0, Time elapsed: 0.062 sec

Results :

Tests run: 1, Failures: 0, Errors: 0, Skipped: 0

[INFO]
[INFO] --- maven-jar-plugin:2.5:jar (default-cli) @ simple-pom-project ---
[INFO] Building jar: C:\projects\apache-maven-cookbook\simple-pom-project\target
\simple-pom-project-1.0-SNAPSHOT.jar
[INFO] ------------------------------------------------------------------------
[INFO] BUILD SUCCESS
[INFO] ------------------------------------------------------------------------
```

We now explicitly invoke the following goals:

▸ `compiler:compile`: This compiles the source files

▸ `compiler:testCompile`: This compiles test files

▸ `surefire:test`: This runs tests

▸ `jar:jar`: This creates a JAR artifact

Maven does not prevent us from doing this.

Running a web project with Jetty

When developing web applications, it is good to have a quick way to check if the application deploys successfully without errors. IDEs allow users to hot-deploy applications. Maven provides a mechanism to quickly run the project using Jetty. Jetty is a popular open source application server that can be used to deploy web projects. The Maven Jetty plugin allows applications to be deployed to Jetty and runs them as part of the Maven build process.

How to do it...

1. Open a simple web project (`simple-web-project`).

2. Run the following Maven command:

   mvn org.eclipse.jetty:jetty-maven-plugin:run

3. Observe the result:

```
Command Prompt - mvn  org.eclipse.jetty:jetty-maven-plugin:run

[INFO]
[INFO] --- jetty-maven-plugin:9.2.1.v20140609:run (default-cli) @ simple-webapp

2014-12-20 07:40:24.460:INFO::main: Logging initialized @2891ms
[INFO] Configuring Jetty for project: simple-webapp Maven Webapp
[INFO] webAppSourceDirectory not set. Trying src\main\webapp
[INFO] Reload Mechanic: automatic
[INFO] Classes = C:\projects\apache-maven-cookbook\simple-webapp\target\classes
[INFO] Context path = /
[INFO] Tmp directory = C:\projects\apache-maven-cookbook\simple-webapp\target\tm
p
[INFO] Web defaults = org/eclipse/jetty/webapp/webdefault.xml
[INFO] Web overrides =  none
[INFO] web.xml file = file:/C:/projects/apache-maven-cookbook/simple-webapp/src/
main/webapp/WEB-INF/web.xml
[INFO] Webapp directory = C:\projects\apache-maven-cookbook\simple-webapp\src\ma
in\webapp
2014-12-20 07:40:24.538:INFO:oejs.Server:main: jetty-9.2.1.v20140609
2014-12-20 07:40:24.976:INFO:/:main: Warning: No org.apache.tomcat.JarScanner se
t in ServletContext. Falling back to default JarScanner implementation.
2014-12-20 07:40:25.226:INFO:oejsh.ContextHandler:main: Started o.e.j.m.p.JettyW
ebAppContext@cf2e646</,file:/C:/projects/apache-maven-cookbook/simple-webapp/src
/main/webapp/,AVAILABLE>{file:/C:/projects/apache-maven-cookbook/simple-webapp/s
rc/main/webapp/>
2014-12-20 07:40:25.226:WARN:oejsh.RequestLogHandler:main: !RequestLog
2014-12-20 07:40:25.257:INFO:oejs.ServerConnector:main: Started ServerConnector@
2aa3873{HTTP/1.1}{0.0.0.0:8080}
2014-12-20 07:40:25.273:INFO:oejs.Server:main: Started @3704ms
[INFO] Started Jetty Server
```

4. Access the web application from the browser by going to `http://localhost:8080`.

How it works...

The Maven Jetty plugin allows web applications to be deployed and tested using Jetty. The `run` goal is bound to the `package` phase. Maven runs all the phases prior to it. Jetty deploys the webapp from its sources; the webapp does not have to be built into a WAR. It looks for the relevant parts of the web application in the default Maven locations. Here are some instances:

- resources in `src/main/webapp`
- classes in `target/classes`
- `web.xml` in `src/main/webapp/WEB-INF`

Jetty uses default values to start the server.

As Jetty is not an official Maven plugin, we have explicitly specified `groupId` (`org.eclipse.jetty`) and `artifactId` (`jetty-maven-plugin`) instead of the short plugin prefix. To use the short plugin prefix, add the following in the settings file:

```
<pluginGroup>org.eclipse.jetty</pluginGroup>
```

Then, Maven can be invoked as follows:

```
mvn jetty:run
```

There's more...

The Maven Jetty plugin provides several goals and configurations to help develop web applications.

1. Run the WAR file:

```
mvn jetty:run-war
```

Jetty now builds the WAR file and then runs it:

```
[INFO] --- jetty-maven-plugin:9.2.1.v20140609:run-war (default-cli) @ simple-web
app ---
2014-12-20 07:58:52.878:INFO::main: Logging initialized @5593ms
[INFO] Configuring Jetty for project: simple-webapp Maven Webapp
[INFO] Context path = /
[INFO] Tmp directory = C:\projects\apache-maven-cookbook\simple-webapp\target\tm
p
[INFO] Web defaults = org/eclipse/jetty/webapp/webdefault.xml
[INFO] Web overrides =  none
2014-12-20 07:58:52.956:INFO:oejs.Server:main: jetty-9.2.1.v20140609
2014-12-20 07:58:53.472:INFO:/:main: Warning: No org.apache.tomcat.JarScanner se
t in ServletContext. Falling back to default JarScanner implementation.
2014-12-20 07:58:53.753:INFO:oejsh.ContextHandler:main: Started o.e.j.m.p.JettyW
ebAppContext@5cYZa526{/,file:/C:/projects/apache-maven-cookbook/simple-webapp/ta
rget/simple-webapp/,AVAILABLE}{C:\projects\apache-maven-cookbook\simple-webapp\t
arget\simple-webapp.war}
2014-12-20 07:58:53.753:WARN:oejsh.RequestLogHandler:main: !RequestLog
```

2. Run the exploded WAR file:

```
mvn jetty:run-exploded
```

Jetty now builds the WAR file, explodes it, and then runs it:

```
2014-12-20 08:03:31.666:INFO:oejs.Server:main: jetty-9.2.1.v20140609
2014-12-20 08:03:32.087:INFO:/:main: Warning: No org.apache.tomcat.JarScanner se
t in ServletContext. Falling back to default JarScanner implementation.
2014-12-20 08:03:32.369:INFO:oejsh.ContextHandler:main: Started o.e.j.m.p.JettyW
ebAppContext@1516d73d{/,file:/C:/projects/apache-maven-cookbook/simple-webapp/ta
rget/simple-webapp/,AVAILABLE}{C:\projects\apache-maven-cookbook\simple-webapp\t
arget\simple-webapp}
2014-12-20 08:03:32.369:WARN:oejsh.RequestLogHandler:main: !RequestLog
```

There are some other goals that can be used as well:

- `jetty:deploy-war`: This deploys an existing WAR file without building it
- `jetty:start`: This starts the Jetty server
- `jetty:stop`: This stops the Jetty server
- `jetty:run-forked`: This runs the Jetty server in a Java virtual machine process different from Maven

Running a web project with Tomcat

Tomcat is a popular open source application server. The Maven Tomcat plugin supports the ability to build and deploy Maven projects in Tomcat. In fact, there are two Maven Tomcat plugins, one for Tomcat 6 and another for Tomcat 7.

Let us look at how to run a web project with Tomcat 7. The steps will be identical for Tomcat 6, except that the plugin would be `tomcat6-maven-plugin` instead of `tomcat7-maven-plugin`, and the plugin prefix would be `tomcat6` instead of `tomcat7`.

How to do it...

1. Open a simple web project (`simple-web-project`).

2. Run the following Maven command:

    `mvn org.apache.tomcat.maven:tomcat7-maven-plugin:run`

3. Observe the result:

```
[INFO] <<< tomcat7-maven-plugin:2.1:run (default-cli) < process-classes @ simple
-webapp <<<
[INFO]
[INFO] --- tomcat7-maven-plugin:2.1:run (default-cli) @ simple-webapp ---
[INFO] Running war on http://localhost:8080/simple-webapp
[INFO] Creating Tomcat server configuration at C:\projects\apache-maven-cookbook
\simple-webapp\target\tomcat
[INFO] create webapp with contextPath: /simple-webapp
Dec 20, 2014 2:51:49 PM org.apache.coyote.AbstractProtocol init
INFO: Initializing ProtocolHandler ["http-bio-8080"]
Dec 20, 2014 2:51:49 PM org.apache.catalina.core.StandardService startInternal
INFO: Starting service Tomcat
Dec 20, 2014 2:51:49 PM org.apache.catalina.core.StandardEngine startInternal
INFO: Starting Servlet Engine: Apache Tomcat/7.0.37
Dec 20, 2014 2:51:50 PM org.apache.coyote.AbstractProtocol start
INFO: Starting ProtocolHandler ["http-bio-8080"]
```

4. Browse to the deployed webapp by visiting `http://localhost:8080/simple-webapp`:

How it works...

The Maven Tomcat plugin allows web applications to be deployed and tested using Apache Tomcat. The `run` goal is bound to the `package` phase. Maven runs all the phases prior to it.

Tomcat uses default values to start the server.

As this is not an official Maven plugin, we have explicitly specified the groupId (`org.apache.tomcat.maven`) and the artifactId (`tomcat7-maven-plugin`) instead of the short plugin prefix. To use the short plugin prefix, add the following in the settings file:

```
<pluginGroup>org.apache.tomcat.maven</pluginGroup>
```

Then Maven can be invoked as follows:

```
mvn tomcat7:run
```

There's more...

The Maven Tomcat7 plugin also supports goals to start and stop Tomcat, which can be used when running integration tests.

It also supports the creation of an executable JAR using embedded Tomcat. Let us see how to do this:

1. Open the web project for which you want to create an executable JAR (`project-with-executable-webapp`).

2. Add the following plugin and configuration:

```
<plugins>
  <plugin>
    <groupId>org.apache.tomcat.maven</groupId>
    <artifactId>tomcat7-maven-plugin</artifactId>
    <version>2.1</version>
    <executions>
      <execution>
        <id>tomcat-run</id>
        <goals>
          <goal>exec-war-only</goal>
        </goals>
        <phase>package</phase>
        <configuration>
          <path>/</path>
        </configuration>
      </execution>
    </executions>
  </plugin>
</plugins>
```

3. Run the following command:

    mvn clean package

4. Run the JAR created in the `target` folder:

   java -jar project-with-executable-webapp-1.0-SNAPSHOT-war-exec.jar

5. Observe the output:

```
C:\projects\apache-maven-cookbook\project-with-executable-webapp\target>java -ja
r project-with-executable-webapp-1.0-SNAPSHOT-war-exec.jar
Dec 20, 2014 3:40:16 PM org.apache.coyote.AbstractProtocol init
INFO: Initializing ProtocolHandler ["http-bio-8080"]
Dec 20, 2014 3:40:16 PM org.apache.catalina.core.StandardService startInternal
INFO: Starting service Tomcat
Dec 20, 2014 3:40:16 PM org.apache.catalina.core.StandardEngine startInternal
INFO: Starting Servlet Engine: Apache Tomcat/7.0.37
Dec 20, 2014 3:40:18 PM org.apache.catalina.util.SessionIdGenerator createSecure
Random
INFO: Creation of SecureRandom instance for session ID generation using [SHA1PRN
G] took [171] milliseconds.
Dec 20, 2014 3:40:18 PM org.apache.coyote.AbstractProtocol start
INFO: Starting ProtocolHandler ["http-bio-8080"]
```

What we have now is a distributable web application using embedded Tomcat.

There is a bug due to which we need to use version 2.1 of the plugin rather than 2.2 for this to work.

11

Advanced Maven Usage

Let us look at the following recipes in this chapter:

- ▸ Creating an assembly
- ▸ Running a custom executable
- ▸ Running an ANT task
- ▸ Determining updates to Maven plugins
- ▸ Determining updates to Maven dependencies
- ▸ Controlling the constraints
- ▸ Generating unique builds
- ▸ Releasing a Maven project

Introduction

In this chapter, we look at using features of Maven that may not be required on a regular basis or for projects. These range from assembling your project for distribution to releasing your project. These are not typical build tasks, but essential elements of a project lifecycle.

Creating an assembly

A typical project requirement is to aggregate the project output along with its dependencies, modules, and other files into a single distributable archive. An assembly is a group of files, directories, and dependencies that are assembled into an archive format and distributed. Maven provides prefabricated assembly descriptors to build these assemblies. The descriptors handle common operations, such as packaging a project's artifact, along with the dependencies.

Getting ready

Maven should be set up on your system and verified to work. To do this, refer to *Chapter 1, Getting Started*.

How to do it...

1. Open a Maven project for which you want to generate the assembly; in our case, `project-with-assembly`.

2. Add the following plugin and configuration to the pom file:

```
<plugin>
  <artifactId>maven-assembly-plugin</artifactId>
  <version>2.5.3</version>
  <configuration>
    <descriptorRefs>
      <descriptorRef>jar-with-dependencies</descriptorRef>
    </descriptorRefs>
    <archive>
      <manifest>
        <mainClass>com.packt.cookbook.App</mainClass>
      </manifest>
    </archive>
  </configuration>
  <executions>
    <execution>
      <id>make-assembly</id>
      <phase>package</phase>
      <goals>
        <goal>single</goal>
      </goals>
    </execution>
  </executions>
</plugin>
```

3. Run the following Maven command:

   `mvn clean package`

4. Observe the output:

   `[INFO] --- maven-assembly-plugin:2.5.3:single (make-assembly) @ project-with-assembly ---`

   `[INFO] Building jar: C:\projects\apache-maven-cookbook\project-with-assembly\target\project-with-assembly-1.0-SNAPSHOT-jar-with-dependencies.jar`

5. Run the created distribution JAR:

```
C:\projects\apache-maven-cookbook\project-with-assembly\
target>java -jar project-with-assembly-1.0-SNAPSHOT-jar-with-
dependencies.jar

07:13:25.660 [main] INFO  com.packt.cookbook.App - Hello World
```

How it works...

We made the following changes to the pom file:

> We chose `jar-with-dependencies`, one of the prefabricated assembly descriptors provided by the Maven Assembly plugin. This creates a single JAR with all the dependencies of the project.

> We also used the `archive` configuration to specify the main class of the project. This is to make the JAR file executable.

> We then specified when the single goal of assembly should be run, namely, the `package` phase.

When Maven ran, it used the preceding configurations to assemble a JAR with dependencies in the package phase. We could run this as a normal executable JAR.

Besides predefined descriptors, the Maven Assembly plugin also allows us to create custom descriptors that can have fine-grained control over the contents of the assembly.

The Assembly plugin can also build an assembly from a multi-module project, where the modules can be part of the final assembly.

There's more...

While opening the JAR file, you would have observed that all the dependant JARs have been unpacked as well.

Name	Size	Packed Size	Modified	Created	Accessed
C:\projects\apache-maven-cookbook\project-with-assembly\target\project-with-assembly-1.0-SNAPSHOT-jar-with-dependencies.jar\					
ch	1 296 575	582 064	2014-04-02 14:10		
com	623	382	2015-02-28 08:09		
META-INF	22 492	5 542	2015-02-28 08:09		
org	64 889	27 944	2014-12-16 22:57		

This is due to the default configuration for the predefined descriptor. Let us see how to create the same distribution but retain dependant JARs as they are. To do this, we will now use one Maven JAR plugin, which uses a custom class loader to load dependant JARs within the parent JAR:

1. Open the project for which you want to create an executable with unpackaged dependant jars (`project-with-one-jar`).

2. Add the following plugin in the pom file:

```xml
<plugin>
    <groupId>org.dstovall</groupId>
    <artifactId>onejar-maven-plugin</artifactId>
    <version>1.4.4</version>
    <executions>
      <execution>
        <id>make-assembly</id>
        <phase>package</phase>
        <goals>
          <goal>one-jar</goal>
        </goals>
      </execution>
    </executions>
  </plugin>
```

3. Add the JAR plugin to specify the main class for the executable JAR:

```xml
<plugin>
    <groupId>org.apache.maven.plugins</groupId>
    <artifactId>maven-jar-plugin</artifactId>
    <configuration>
    <archive>
        <manifest>
                <mainClass>com.packt.cookbook.App</mainClass>
        </manifest>
      </archive>
    </configuration>
  </plugin>
```

4. Add the following code as the plugin binaries are not in the central Maven repository:

```xml
<pluginRepositories>
    <pluginRepository>
        <id>onejar-maven-plugin.googlecode.com</id>
        <url>http://onejar-maven-plugin.googlecode.com/svn/
mavenrepo</url>
    </pluginRepository>
  </pluginRepositories>
```

5. Run the following command:

```
mvn package
```

6. Run the generated executable and observe the result:

```
java -jar project-with-one-jar-1.0-SNAPSHOT.one-jar.jar
06:57:45.995 [main] INFO  com.packt.cookbook.App - Hello World
```

7. Open the created JAR file:

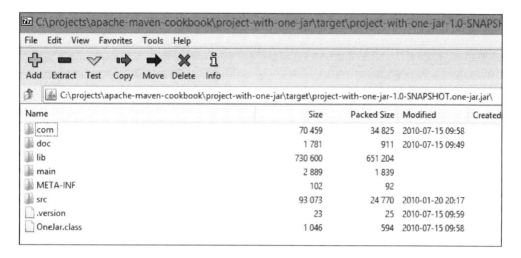

We can see that in contrast to the assembly JAR, the executable JAR is created without unpacking the libraries (dependencies) involved.

8. Navigate to the `lib` folder in the JAR:

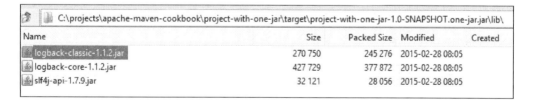

The dependant JARs are stored in the `lib` folder.

See also

▸ The *Generating an executable JAR* recipe in *Chapter 10, Java Development with Maven*

Running a custom executable

There are many situations when you want Maven to run a specific executable on your computer. A simple use case would be to run the JAR that you created. Another case would be to have Maven run commands that are not provided as plugins (for instance, create a native Windows installer).

Maven provides support to run any executable system in a separate process along with Java programs in the same virtual machine on which Maven runs. The Maven Exec plugin provides this support using the `exec` goal (to run in a separate process) and the `java` goal (to run Java programs in the same process).

How to do it...

1. Open a simple Maven project (`simple-project`).

2. Run the command:

   ```
   mvn clean package exec:java -Dexec.mainClass="com.packt.cookbook.
   App"
   ```

3. Observe the results:

   ```
   [INFO]
   [INFO] --- exec-maven-plugin:1.3.2:java (default-cli) @ simple-project ---
   [WARNING] Warning: killAfter is now deprecated. Do you need it ? Please comment
   on MEXEC-6.
   Hello World!
   ```

How it works...

We wanted to run the JAR file that we had created in the project. To do this, we called the `java` goal of the Maven Exec plugin. We provided the plugin with the required parameter (`mainClass`) so that it knew which main class needed to be run.

There's more...

You could integrate the running of the executable as part of the project lifecycle. Let us do this for our example:

1. Open the project (let's call it `project-with-exec`).

2. Add the following code to the pom file:

   ```xml
   <plugin>
       <groupId>org.codehaus.mojo</groupId>
       <artifactId>exec-maven-plugin</artifactId>
       <version>1.3.2</version>
   ```

```
        <executions>
          <execution>
            <id>hello-world</id>
            <phase>package</phase>
            <goals>
              <goal>java</goal>
            </goals>
          </execution>
        </executions>
        <configuration>
          <mainClass>com.packt.cookbook.App</mainClass>
        </configuration>
      </plugin>
```

3. Run the following command:

   mvn clean package

4. Observe the result:

   ```
   [INFO] --- maven-jar-plugin:2.4:jar (default-jar) @ project-with-
   exec ---
   [INFO] Building jar: C:\projects\apache-maven-cookbook\project-
   with-exec\target\
   project-with-exec-1.0-SNAPSHOT.jar
   [INFO]
   [INFO] --- exec-maven-plugin:1.3.2:java (hello-world) @ project-
   with-exec ---
   [WARNING] Warning: killAfter is now deprecated. Do you need it ?
   Please comment
   on MEXEC-6.
   06:25:26.005 [com.packt.cookbook.App.main()] INFO  com.packt.
   cookbook.App - Hell
   o World
   [INFO] ------------------------------------------------------------
   -------------
   ```

The project is run during the package phase based on the configuration that we specified in the plugin.

The same can be done for non-Java executables; we need to invoke the exec goal instead of the java goal.

 Running system executables makes the build nonportable, so use it with care.

Running an ANT task

ANT is a popular build automation tool that provides a great degree of flexibility. It also provides tasks, such as echo and touch, that are not available in Maven. There might be advantages in combining ANT tasks with Maven to achieve certain goals, though it is best to avoid it until it's inevitable.

Maven provides a mechanism to run arbitrary ANT tasks by way of the Maven AntRun plugin. Let us see how to use this to run an ANT task in our project.

How to do it...

1. Open a project for which you want to run ANT tasks (project-with-ant).

2. Add the following plugin configuration to the pom file:

```
<plugin>
    <artifactId>maven-antrun-plugin</artifactId>
    <version>1.8</version>
    <executions>
      <execution>
        <phase>package</phase>
        <configuration>
          <target>
              <echo message="Calling ant task in package
phase"/>
          </target>
        </configuration>
        <goals>
          <goal>run</goal>
        </goals>
      </execution>
    </executions>
</plugin>
```

3. Run the following Maven command:

```
mvn clean package
```

4. Observe the output:

```
[INFO]
[INFO] ---- maven-jar-plugin:2.4:jar (default-jar) @ project-with-ant ----
[INFO] Building jar: C:\projects\apache-maven-cookbook\project-with-ant\target\p
roject-with-ant-1.0-SNAPSHOT.jar
[INFO]
[INFO] ---- maven-antrun-plugin:1.8:run (default) @ project-with-ant ----
[INFO] Executing tasks

main:
     [echo] Calling ant task in package phase
[INFO] Executed tasks
[INFO] ----
```

How it works...

We configured the Maven AntRun plugin to run an ANT target during the package phase. In the ANT target, we specified a simple echo task, which outputted a string we wanted.

Instead of the echo task, we could write more complex tasks. The Maven AntRun plugin also provides a means for ANT tasks to refer to Maven properties, class paths, and others.

There's more...

It is good practice to separate ANT tasks to a separate ANT build script (build.xml) and invoke the same from Maven. Let us see how to do this:

1. Create a simple ANT build script, build.xml, and add the following contents:

```
<project name="project-with-ant" default="echo" basedir=".">
  <description>
      Simple ant task to echo a string
  </description>

  <target name="echo">
      <echo message="Hello World"/>
  </target>
</project>
```

2. Replace the target configuration in the pom file as follows:

```
<target>
    <ant target="echo"/>
  </target>
```

3. Run the Maven command:

mvn clean package

4. Observe the output:

```
[INFO] --- maven-jar-plugin:2.4:jar (default-jar) @ project-with-ant ---
[INFO] Building jar: C:\projects\apache-maven-cookbook\project-with-ant\target\p
roject-with-ant-1.0-SNAPSHOT.jar
[INFO]
[INFO] --- maven-antrun-plugin:1.8:run (default) @ project-with-ant ---
[INFO] Executing tasks

main:

echo:
     [echo] Hello World
[INFO] Executed tasks
[INFO] -----------------------------------------------------------------
```

The result is the same, but now the ANT scripts are separated from Maven.

Determining updates to Maven plugin AntRun

In our build scripts, we explicitly specify the version of the Maven plugins that we use. This is required in order to create reproducible builds. In the absence of the version, Maven gives a warning such as the following:

`[WARNING] Some problems were encountered while building the effective model for`

`com.packt.cookbook:project-with-exec:jar:1.0-SNAPSHOT`

`[WARNING] 'build.plugins.plugin.version' for org.codehaus.mojo:exec-maven-plugin is missing. @ line 42, column 17`

`[WARNING]`

`[WARNING] It is highly recommended to fix these problems because they threaten the stability of your build.`

`[WARNING]`

`[WARNING] For this reason, future Maven versions might no longer support building such malformed projects.`

Over a period of time, there could be updates to these plugins. It would be good to know if there are any so that we can suitably update the plugin versions. Let us see how we can do this.

How to do it...

1. Take a project for which you want to check the plugin update (`project-with-exec`).

2. Change the version of the plugin to an older one:

   ```
   <artifactId>exec-maven-plugin</artifactId>
     <version>1.2</version>>
   ```

3. Run the following command:

    ```
    mvn versions:display-plugin-updates
    ```

4. Observe the output:

    ```
    [INFO] --- versions-maven-plugin:2.0:display-plugin-updates
    (default-cli) @ proj
    ect-with-exec ---
    [INFO]
    [INFO] All plugins with a version specified are using the latest
    versions.
    ...
    [WARNING] The following plugins do not have their version
    specified:
    [WARNING]   maven-clean-plugin ......................... (from
    super-pom) 2.5
    [WARNING]   maven-compiler-plugin ...................... (from
    super-pom) 3.1
    ...
    [WARNING] Project does not define minimum Maven version, default
    is: 2.0
    [INFO] Plugins require minimum Maven version of: 2.2.1
    ...
    [ERROR] Project does not define required minimum version of Maven.
    [ERROR] Update the pom.xml to contain
    [ERROR]       <prerequisites>
    [ERROR]           <maven>2.2.1</maven>
    [ERROR]       </prerequisites>
    ...
    [INFO] Require Maven 2.2.1 to use the following plugin updates:
    [INFO]   maven-jar-plugin ........................................
    ........ 2.5
    [INFO]   maven-site-plugin .......................................
    ........ 3.2
    [INFO]   org.codehaus.mojo:exec-maven-plugin
    ........................... 1.3.2
    ```

How it works...

The `display-plugin-updates` goal of the Maven Versions plugin downloads the metadata for all the plugins specified in the pom file and then produces a report. The report reveals a number of things that are of interest.

▶ A `prerequisites` tag is absent. The `prerequisites` tag in the pom file specifies the minimum version of Maven that is required to build the project. In the absence of this, Maven takes the minimum version as `2.0`. There is a risk of nonreproducible builds if different developers use different versions of Maven. Hence, it is a good practice to specify a minimum version by using this tag.

▶ There is a warning about plugin versions not being defined. As we have seen, plugins in the pom file don't need to be specified explicitly unless they need to be configured. Now, Maven still uses various plugins for execution (such as clean, resources, compile, test, and so on) and it needs to determine the version to be used. It uses the version specified by the super pom, which is fine in most cases. However, the Versions plugin alerts us that this is the case, so we can take action as appropriate.

▶ There is a difference in plugin versions based on the Maven version. The report specifies different versions of various plugins based on the Maven version used. This is all the more reason why it is important to specify a prerequisite.

As the output indicates, if we specify that we need at least the `2.2.1` version of Maven, then we can see that there is a newer version of the Maven Exec plugin, which is `1.3.2`.

There's more...

Let us now specify the `prerequisites` element in the pom file and see how it affects the output of the goal:

1. Add the following to the pom file:

   ```
   <prerequisites>
     <maven>3.2.5</maven>
   </prerequisites>
   ```

2. Run the following command:

   `mvn versions:display-plugin-updates`

3. Observe the output:

   `[INFO] --- versions-maven-plugin:2.0:display-plugin-updates (default-cli) @ project-with-exec ---`

   `...`

   `INFO]`

```
INFO] The following plugin updates are available:
INFO]    org.codehaus.mojo:exec-maven-plugin .....................
1.2 -> 1.3.2
INFO]
```

We now see that the plugin reports a plugin update based on the prerequisite that we specified.

It is difficult to determine if there are updates to plugins that we do not explicitly define in the pom file. For instance, as per the output from the preceding command, which is as follows:

```
[WARNING] The following plugins do not have their version
specified:
[WARNING]    maven-clean-plugin ......................... (from
super-pom) 2.5
[WARNING]    maven-compiler-plugin ...................... (from
super-pom) 3.1
[WARNING]    maven-deploy-plugin ........................ (from
super-pom) 2.7
[WARNING]    maven-install-plugin ....................... (from
super-pom) 2.4
```

However, as of writing this book, the latest version of the Maven Clean plugin is 2.6.1, that of the Maven Compiler plugin is 3.2, and so on. The version that the super pom has is the version that must have been the latest when it was created. The versions of these dependencies become important when bugs or newer features are present in the newer versions. In this case, we do want to get the newer version of these plugins. It is easy to get these by explicitly specifying the version of the plugins in the pom file.

Add the following to the pom file:

```
<plugin>
    <groupId>org.apache.maven.plugins</groupId>
    <artifactId>maven-clean-plugin</artifactId>
    <version>2.5</version>
</plugin>
<plugin>
    <groupId>org.apache.maven.plugins</groupId>
    <artifactId>maven-compiler-plugin</artifactId>
    <version>3.1</version>
</plugin>
```

Now, re-run the previous command and note the output:

```
[INFO] The following plugin updates are available:
[INFO]    maven-clean-plugin ..................................... 2.5 ->
2.6.1
[INFO]    maven-compiler-plugin ................................. 3.1
-> 3.2
[INFO]    org.codehaus.mojo:exec-maven-plugin ................... 1.2 ->
1.3.2
```

Determining updates to Maven dependencies

We use a number of third-party libraries to build our projects. As you recall, we specify the groupId, artifactId, and version elements of each of these dependant libraries in our pom file. There may be many occasions when there are updates to these libraries and new versions are released. It will be good to have a mechanism to get notified about these releases and update the project build file suitably.

How to do it...

1. Take a project for which you want to check for a dependency update, simple-project, which we had created using the quick-start archetype.

2. Run the following command:

   ```
   mvn versions:display-dependency-updates
   ```

3. Observe the output:

   ```
   [INFO] --- versions-maven-plugin:2.1:display-dependency-updates
   (default-cli) @
   simple-project ---
   [INFO] artifact junit:junit: checking for updates from central
   [INFO] The following dependencies in Dependencies have newer
   versions:
   [INFO]    junit:junit ...........................................
   3.8.1 -> 4.12
   ```

How it works...

The `display-dependency-updates` goal of the Maven Versions plugin uses the metadata of each of the maven dependencies to determine the latest version of each dependency. If it does not match the current version, it displays a report about the difference.

We have already seen earlier that `SNAPSHOT` versions are handled differently by Maven, and it automatically checks and updates these dependencies for each build as per the configuration. If the version number of the `SNAPSHOT` changes (`1.0-SNAPSHOT` to `1.1-SNAPSHOT`), then the Versions plugin indicates that.

There's more...

The Maven Versions plugin provides several other goals to manage updates to dependency and plugin versions. This includes automatically changing the versions to the latest release versions, replacing `SNAPSHOT` with release versions, and so on.

Controlling the constraints

One of the requirements for a build tool is to be able to generate repeatable builds. In a project, the build tool should behave identically for all team members. While a project guideline can be made on the version of Java or Maven to be used, it would be easier if it could be enforced automatically.

This is where the Maven Enforcer plugin comes in.

How to do it...

1. Open a simple project (`project-with-enforcer`).

2. Add the following plugin configuration:

```
<plugin>
  <groupId>org.apache.maven.plugins</groupId>
  <artifactId>maven-enforcer-plugin</artifactId>
  <version>1.3.1</version>
  <executions>
    <execution>
      <id>enforce-versions</id>
      <goals>
        <goal>enforce</goal>
      </goals>
      <configuration>
```

```
            <rules>
              <requireMavenVersion>
                <version>3.2.3</version>
              </requireMavenVersion>
              <requireJavaVersion>
                <version>1.8</version>
              </requireJavaVersion>
            </rules>
          </configuration>
        </execution>
      </executions>
    </plugin>
```

3. Build the project using Java 7 and Maven 3.2.3:

    mvn clean package.

4. Observe the output:

```
[INFO] ----    maven-enforcer-plugin:1.3.1:enforce (enforce-versions) @ project-with
-enforcer ----
[WARNING] Rule 0: org.apache.maven.plugins.enforcer.RequireMavenVersion failed w
ith message:
Detected Maven Version: 3.2.3 is not in the allowed range 3.2.5.
[WARNING] Rule 1: org.apache.maven.plugins.enforcer.RequireJavaVersion failed wi
th message:
Detected JDK Version: 1.7.0-67 is not in the allowed range 1.8.
[INFO] ------------------------------------------------------------------------
[INFO] BUILD FAILURE
[INFO] ------------------------------------------------------------------------
[INFO] Total time: 0.821 s
[INFO] Finished at: 2015-01-12T06:36:26+05:30
[INFO] Final Memory: 6M/154M
[INFO] ------------------------------------------------------------------------
[ERROR] Failed to execute goal org.apache.maven.plugins:maven-enforcer-plugin:1.
3.1:enforce (enforce-versions) on project project-with-enforcer: Some Enforcer r
ules have failed. Look above for specific messages explaining why the rule faile
d. -> [Help 1]
[ERROR]
```

How it works...

The Enforcer plugin uses the rules configuration and validates the project against the rules. If it finds violations, it reports the error(s) and does not proceed with the build.

In the preceding example, our project had two issues:

▶ **The Maven version**: We were using version 3.2.3 but we had specified 3.2.5 in the rules

▶ **The Java version**: We were using Java 7 but we had specified Java 8 in the rules

There's more...

The Maven Enforcer plugin has several other rules to enforce various constraints. A couple of them are as follows:

- `requireOS`: This ensures the project can be built only on specific operating systems
- `requireFilesExist`: This ensures specific files exist for the project to build

It is also possible to implement custom enforcer rules. One such is available at `https://github.com/ferstl/pedantic-pom-enforcers`.

Generating unique builds

As we have seen, we use a `SNAPSHOT` version to specify that the project is under development. In the course of development, we will create several builds for the project. In many situations, it will be useful to distinguish one such build from another. One could be when we use continuous integration. Another would be when a tester needs to log defects against a build.

It would be nice if there was a way to generate a unique build number to identify a build in the case of `SNAPSHOT` versions.

How to do it...

1. Open the project for which you want to have a build number (`project-with-build-number`).

2. Add the following plugin configuration:

```xml
<plugin>
    <groupId>org.codehaus.mojo</groupId>
    <artifactId>buildnumber-maven-plugin</artifactId>
    <version>1.3</version>
    <executions>
      <execution>
        <phase>validate</phase>
        <goals>
          <goal>create</goal>
        </goals>
      </execution>
    </executions>
    <configuration>
      <shortRevisionLength>5</shortRevisionLength>
```

```
        </configuration>
    </plugin>
```

3. Add the following to use the unique build number created:

```
<finalName>${project.artifactId}-${project.version}-
r${buildNumber}</finalName>
```

4. Add the SCM configuration for the project:

```
<scm>
      <developerConnection>scm:git:https://bitbucket.org/maruhgar/
apache-maven-cookbook</developerConnection>
          <url>https://bitbucket.org/maruhgar/apache-maven-cookbook</
url>
    </scm>
```

5. Build the project:

    mvn clean package

6. Observe the output:

    [INFO] --- buildnumber-maven-plugin:1.3:create (default) @ project-with-build-nu

    mber ---

    [INFO] ShortRevision tag detected. The value is '5'.

    [INFO] Executing: cmd.exe /X /C "git rev-parse --verify --short=5 HEAD"

    [INFO] Working directory: C:\projects\apache-maven-cookbook\ project-with-build-n

    umber

    [INFO] Storing buildNumber: 0950d at timestamp: 1421244408851

    [INFO] Storing buildScmBranch: master

    ...

    [INFO] --- maven-jar-plugin:2.4:jar (default-jar) @ project-with-build-number --

    -

    [INFO] Building jar: C:\projects\apache-maven-cookbook\project-with-build-number

    \target\project-with-build-number-1.0-SNAPSHOT-r0950d.jar

How it works...

The Maven Build Number plugin provides three ways to generate a unique number, namely by using SCM, a sequential build number, or a timestamp.

In the preceding example, we used SCM as it is easy to map the build against the corresponding SCM version. We used `git` and specified the SCM details in the SCM tag of the pom file.

We also specified to the Maven Build Number plugin to use five characters and create the short revision, as a typical git revision is a long hash value. We also configured the plugin to run during the validation phase of the lifecycle.

We used the generated Build Number in the name of the generated artifact, by appending it along with the version number.

Now, each time a new check-in is done and the build is completed, an artifact with a unique name is generated. Based on the requirement, each such artifact can be archived or traced to a corresponding source.

Releasing a Maven project

The ultimate goal of any project is the release. After development is complete and bugs are fixed, it is time to release the project. Different projects are released in different ways. Web projects are released by deploying them to the web server. Other projects may be packaged into executable JARs. Still others may be packaged as executables or installers. If the project is a library or a dependency used in other projects, then it needs to be made available suitably.

As we have seen before, we use the SNAPSHOT version during development. When the project has to be released, this version now needs to be replaced with a concrete version.

One of the most advanced features of Maven is its support to do a project release. Let us explore this.

How to do it...

1. Open a project for which you want to do a release (`project-with-release`).
2. Verify if the SCM details are present in the pom file:

```
<scm>
      <developerConnection>scm:git:https://bitbucket.org/maruhgar/
apache-maven-cookbook</developerConnection>
      <url>https://bitbucket.org/maruhgar/apache-maven-cookbook</
url>
```

```
      <tag>HEAD</tag>
   </scm>
```

3. Add the plugin definition in order to specify the latest version of the plugin:

```
<plugins>
   <plugin>
      <groupId>org.apache.maven.plugins</groupId>
      <artifactId>maven-release-plugin</artifactId>
      <version>2.5.1</version>
   </plugin>
</plugins>
```

4. Run the following Maven command:

   mvn release:prepare -DpushChanges=false

   By default, changes made by the plugin are pushed to the repository. If you do not want that, set the `pushChanges` configuration option to `false`.

5. Choose the default values when prompted.

```
C:\projects\apache-maven-cookbook\project-with-release>mvn release:prepare -Dpus
hChanges=false
[INFO] Scanning for projects...
[INFO]
[INFO] ------------------------------------------------------------------------
[INFO] Building Project with release 1.0-SNAPSHOT
[INFO] ------------------------------------------------------------------------
[INFO]
[INFO]
[INFO] --- maven-release-plugin:2.5.1:prepare (default-cli) @ project-with-relea
se ---
[INFO] Verifying that there are no local modifications...
[INFO]   ignoring changes on: **\pom.xml.next, **\release.properties, **\pom.xml
.branch, **\pom.xml.tag, **\pom.xml.backup, **\pom.xml.releaseBackup
[INFO] Executing: cmd.exe /X /C "git status"
[INFO] Working directory: C:\projects\apache-maven-cookbook\project-with-release

[INFO] Checking dependencies and plugins for snapshots ...
What is the release version for "Project with release"? (com.packt.cookbook:proj
ect-with-release) 1.0: :
What is SCM release tag or label for "Project with release"? (com.packt.cookbook
:project-with-release) project-with-release-1.0: :
What is the new development version for "Project with release"? (com.packt.cookb
ook:project-with-release) 1.1-SNAPSHOT: :
[INFO] Transforming 'Project with release'...
[INFO] Not generating release POMs
[INFO] Executing goals 'clean verify'...
```

You could choose the default values for the release version, the SCM tag and new development version, or provide your values.

6. Observe the output:

```
[INFO] [INFO] ------------------------------------------------------------
[INFO] Checking in modified POMs...
[INFO] Executing: cmd.exe /X /C "git add -- pom.xml"
[INFO] Working directory: C:\projects\apache-maven-cookbook\project-with-release

[INFO] Executing: cmd.exe /X /C "git rev-parse --show-toplevel"
[INFO] Working directory: C:\projects\apache-maven-cookbook\project-with-release

[INFO] Executing: cmd.exe /X /C "git status --porcelain ."
[INFO] Working directory: C:\projects\apache-maven-cookbook\project-with-release

[WARNING] Ignoring unrecognized line: ?? project-with-release/pom.xml.releaseBac
kup
[WARNING] Ignoring unrecognized line: ?? project-with-release/release.properties

[INFO] Executing: cmd.exe /X /C "git commit --verbose -F C:\Users\raghu\AppData\
Local\Temp\maven-scm-1831156722.commit pom.xml"
[INFO] Working directory: C:\projects\apache-maven-cookbook\project-with-release

[INFO] Tagging release with the label project-with-release-1.0...
[INFO] Executing: cmd.exe /X /C "git tag -F C:\Users\raghu\AppData\Local\Temp\ma
ven-scm-911129703.commit project-with-release-1.0"
[INFO] Working directory: C:\projects\apache-maven-cookbook\project-with-release

[INFO] Executing: cmd.exe /X /C "git ls-files"
[INFO] Working directory: C:\projects\apache-maven-cookbook\project-with-release

[INFO] Transforming 'Project with release'...
[INFO] Not removing release POMs
[INFO] Checking in modified POMs...
[INFO] Executing: cmd.exe /X /C "git add -- pom.xml"
[INFO] Working directory: C:\projects\apache-maven-cookbook\project-with-release

[INFO] Executing: cmd.exe /X /C "git rev-parse --show-toplevel"
[INFO] Working directory: C:\projects\apache-maven-cookbook\project-with-release

[INFO] Executing: cmd.exe /X /C "git status --porcelain ."
[INFO] Working directory: C:\projects\apache-maven-cookbook\project-with-release

[WARNING] Ignoring unrecognized line: ?? project-with-release/pom.xml.releaseBac
kup
[WARNING] Ignoring unrecognized line: ?? project-with-release/release.properties

[INFO] Executing: cmd.exe /X /C "git commit --verbose -F C:\Users\raghu\AppData\
Local\Temp\maven-scm-1435754747.commit pom.xml"
[INFO] Working directory: C:\projects\apache-maven-cookbook\project-with-release

[INFO] Release preparation complete.
[INFO] ------------------------------------------------------------
```

Maven runs a number of commands that modify the pom file. Then, it checks in the changes into the repository.

7. Now run the following command:

```
mvn release:perform -Dgoals=package -DlocalCheckout=true
```

By default, the `perform` goal of the Maven Release plugin runs the `deploy` goal to deploy the project to the specified repository. If you do not have a remote repository to deploy to, or want to run a different goal as part of the release, you can specify it using the `goals` configuration. In the preceding case, we have set it to run the `package` goal.

Also, to do the release, Maven checks out the tag created by the `prepare` goal from the repository. If you want Maven to check out the local copy instead, you could do so by setting the `localCheckout` configuration to `true`.

8. Observe the output:

```
C:\projects\apache-maven-cookbook\project-with-release>mvn release:perform -Dgoal
ls=package -DlocalCheckout=true
[INFO] Scanning for projects...
[INFO]
[INFO]
[INFO] ------------------------------------------------------------------------
[INFO] Building Project with release 1.1-SNAPSHOT
[INFO] ------------------------------------------------------------------------
[INFO]
[INFO]
[INFO] --- maven-release-plugin:2.5.1:perform (default-cli) @ project-with-relea
se ---
[INFO] Performing a LOCAL checkout from scm:git:file:///C:\projects\apache-maven
-cookbook\project-with-release
[INFO] Checking out the project to perform the release ...
[INFO] Executing: cmd.exe /X /C "git clone --branch project-with-release-1.0 fil
e:///C:\projects\apache-maven-cookbook\project-with-release C:\projects\apache-m
aven-cookbook\project-with-release\target\checkout"
[INFO] Working directory: C:\projects\apache-maven-cookbook\project-with-release
\target
[INFO] Performing a LOCAL checkout from scm:git:file:///C:\projects\apache-maven
-cookbook
[INFO] Checking out the project to perform the release ...
[INFO] Executing: cmd.exe /X /C "git clone --branch project-with-release-1.0 fil
e:///C:\projects\apache-maven-cookbook C:\projects\apache-maven-cookbook\project
-with-release\target\checkout"
[INFO] Working directory: C:\projects\apache-maven-cookbook\project-with-release
\target
[INFO] Executing: cmd.exe /X /C "git ls-remote file:///C:\projects\apache-maven-
cookbook"
[INFO] Working directory: C:\Users\raghu\AppData\Local\Temp
[INFO] Executing: cmd.exe /X /C "git fetch file:///C:\projects\apache-maven-cook
book"
[INFO] Working directory: C:\projects\apache-maven-cookbook\project-with-release
\target\checkout
[INFO] Executing: cmd.exe /X /C "git checkout project-with-release-1.0"
[INFO] Working directory: C:\projects\apache-maven-cookbook\project-with-release
\target\checkout
[INFO] Executing: cmd.exe /X /C "git ls-files"
[INFO] Working directory: C:\projects\apache-maven-cookbook\project-with-release
\target\checkout
[INFO] Invoking perform goals in directory C:\projects\apache-maven-cookbook\pro
ject-with-release\target\checkout\project-with-release
[INFO] Executing goals 'package'...
```

9. Ensure that the release binaries are created in the `target/checkout/project-with-release/target` folder:

```
C:\projects\apache-maven-cookbook\project-with-release\target\checkout\proj
ith-release\target>dir
 Volume in drive C has no label.
 Volume Serial Number is 04B8-E184

 Directory of C:\projects\apache-maven-cookbook\project-with-release\target
kout\project-with-release\target

15-01-2015  13:03    <DIR>          .
15-01-2015  13:03    <DIR>          ..
15-01-2015  13:03    <DIR>          apidocs
15-01-2015  13:03    <DIR>          classes
15-01-2015  13:03    <DIR>          javadoc-bundle-options
15-01-2015  13:03    <DIR>          maven-archiver
15-01-2015  13:03    <DIR>          maven-status
15-01-2015  13:03            23,214 project-with-release-1.0-javadoc.jar
15-01-2015  13:03               903 project-with-release-1.0-sources.jar
15-01-2015  13:03             2,524 project-with-release-1.0.jar
15-01-2015  13:03    <DIR>          surefire-reports
15-01-2015  13:03    <DIR>          test-classes
```

How it works...

There are two steps to making a release—prepare and perform.

When the prepare goal of the Maven Release plugin is run, it does the following:

- Checks there are no uncommitted changes
- Checks that the project does not have any SNAPSHOT dependencies
- Changes the version of the SNAPSHOT project; you will be prompted to confirm or override the default
- Adds a tag element to the scm element and computes the value (by default, HEAD)
- Runs the verify goal to ensure that the changes do not break anything
- Commits the modified pom to the SCM
- Tags the code in SCM with a version name (you will be prompted to confirm or override the default):

```
commit 7dc92717f16ca69477fff01156bc7292f09a9ca9
Author: Raghuram Bharathan <raghu@i            .com>
Date:    Thu Jan 15 12:51:33 2015 +0530

    [maven-release-plugin] prepare for next development iteration

commit cea5883c64c82d9cdd7e08aa80600ee0a58b14e9
Author: Raghuram Bharathan <raghu@i            .com>
Date:    Thu Jan 15 12:51:32 2015 +0530

    [maven-release-plugin] prepare release project-with-release-1.0
```

- Bumps the version in the pom to the new SNAPSHOT value (from 1.0-SNAPSHOT; this would be 1.1-SNAPSHOT); you will be prompted to confirm or override this
- Commits the modified pom to SCM

As you can see, once the goal is met, you will have an updated SCM with a tag with the release version and the HEAD with the next SNAPSHOT version. A release.properties file is also created. It contains information that is needed for the perform goal.

```
C:\projects\apache-maven-cookbook\project-with-release>dir
 Volume in drive C has no label.
 Volume Serial Number is 04B8-E184

 Directory of C:\projects\apache-maven-cookbook\project-with-release

14-01-2015  20:19    <DIR>          .
14-01-2015  20:19    <DIR>          ..
14-01-2015  20:17               909 pom.xml
14-01-2015  20:16               891 pom.xml.releaseBackup
14-01-2015  20:17               842 release.properties
14-01-2015  20:02    <DIR>          src
14-01-2015  20:17    <DIR>          target
               3 File(s)          2,642 bytes
```

The second platform does as follows:

- The perform goal uses the information in `release.properties` to check out from the SCM tag that was created earlier
- It then runs the specified goal on the checked-out project (by default, `deploy`)
- This generates the release binaries

Once the build is successful, `release.properties` and other backup files created by the Release plugin are removed.

Index

U

V

W

Thank you for buying
Apache Maven Cookbook

About Packt Publishing

Packt, pronounced 'packed', published its first book, *Mastering phpMyAdmin for Effective MySQL Management*, in April 2004, and subsequently continued to specialize in publishing highly focused books on specific technologies and solutions.

Our books and publications share the experiences of your fellow IT professionals in adapting and customizing today's systems, applications, and frameworks. Our solution-based books give you the knowledge and power to customize the software and technologies you're using to get the job done. Packt books are more specific and less general than the IT books you have seen in the past. Our unique business model allows us to bring you more focused information, giving you more of what you need to know, and less of what you don't.

Packt is a modern yet unique publishing company that focuses on producing quality, cutting-edge books for communities of developers, administrators, and newbies alike. For more information, please visit our website at www.packtpub.com.

About Packt Open Source

In 2010, Packt launched two new brands, Packt Open Source and Packt Enterprise, in order to continue its focus on specialization. This book is part of the Packt open source brand, home to books published on software built around open source licenses, and offering information to anybody from advanced developers to budding web designers. The Open Source brand also runs Packt's open source Royalty Scheme, by which Packt gives a royalty to each open source project about whose software a book is sold.

Writing for Packt

We welcome all inquiries from people who are interested in authoring. Book proposals should be sent to author@packtpub.com. If your book idea is still at an early stage and you would like to discuss it first before writing a formal book proposal, then please contact us; one of our commissioning editors will get in touch with you.

We're not just looking for published authors; if you have strong technical skills but no writing experience, our experienced editors can help you develop a writing career, or simply get some additional reward for your expertise.

Maven Build Customization

ISBN: 978-1-78398-722-1   Paperback: 270 pages

Discover the real power of Maven 3 to manage your Java projects more effectively than ever

1. Administer complex projects customizing the Maven framework and improving the software lifecycle of your organization with "Maven friend technologies".

2. Automate your delivery process and make it fast and easy.

3. An easy-to-follow tutorial on Maven customization and integration with a real project and practical examples.

Apache Maven 3 Cookbook

ISBN: 978-1-84951-244-2   Paperback: 224 pages

Over 50 recipes towards optimal Java software engineering with Maven 3

1. Grasp the fundamentals and extend Apache Maven 3 to meet your needs.

2. Implement engineering practices in your application development process with Apache Maven.

3. Collaboration techniques for Agile teams with Apache Maven.

Please check **www.PacktPub.com** for information on our titles

Learning Apache Maven 3 [Video]

ISBN: 978-1-78216-666-5   Duration: 01:59 hours

Get to grips with the basics and concepts of building a real world Java Application with Apache Maven

1. A practical example-driven approach to learning Apache Maven 3.

2. Grasp the fundamentals and extend Apache Maven 3 to meet your needs.

3. Learn to use Apache Maven with Java, Enterprise Frameworks, and various other cutting-edge technologies.

Apache Maven Dependency Management

ISBN: 978-1-78328-301-9   Paperback: 158 pages

Manage your Java and JEE project dependencies with ease with this hands-on guide to Maven

1. Improve your productivity by efficiently managing dependencies.

2. Learn how to detect and fix dependency conflicts.

3. Learn how to share transitive relations and to visualize your dependencies.

Please check **www.PacktPub.com** for information on our titles

60500435R00152

Made in the USA
Lexington, KY
08 February 2017